5

St
story
V. 1. 500

THE
SCIENCE OF STORY
BRAND IS A REFLECTION OF CULTURE

ADAM FRIDMAN

HANK OSTHOLTHOFF

The Science of Story

Brand is a Reflection of Culture

ADAM FRIDMAN

HANK OSTHOLTHOFF

Inspired by the Mabbly Tribe

Table of Contents

Foreword

Why does story and purpose matter to you and your organization?

For that answer, we need to look to the storyline that has been emerging in the talent marketplace for over 20 years. In 1997, McKinsey launched the War for Talent. We saw the forecasts that told us of a challenging future—that talent would become hard to find and even harder to hang on to. McKinsey predicted that there would be unprecedented talent shortages in the years to come. It was a time when you could interview in the morning and have an offer by the end of the day if you had the right skill set.

The war for talent ushered in a conversation that was top of mind to C-suite leaders and Human Resource Practitioners. Talent was a top priority and not having the right talent was a significant constraint to growth. When the dot com bubble burst, it seemed like we went from a candidate market for talent to an employer market overnight. Companies pulled back, they were now in the driver's seat. There were takeaways, a significant attempt to adjust starting salaries to a lower level, some organizations reduced benefits, all in a market where jobs were hard to find and candidates were plentiful. Voices in the market at that time referred to it as the employers' revenge, or at the very least, a time to even the score.[1]

People wondered, whatever happened to the war for talent? It didn't go away, it just went underground for a few years. In fact, the advice from insightful companies wasn't to abandon the focus on talent, but to take advantage of the downturn in the market by acquiring great talent at more moderate salaries. As a majority of organizations cut training and

---

[1] Ed Michaels, *The War for Talent* (Boston, Massachusetts: Harvard Business School Publishing, 2001).

development budgets, companies with a clear talent strategy invested in developing their people. As a result, in many cases, their people investments paid big dividends in results and building their pipelines for the future.

We have seen many economic cycles over the last two decades. When we began to come out of the Great Recession of 2007/2008, we heard a lot about jobless recoveries as job creation lagged improved business results. But then, in 2010/2011, we started to see a gradual uptick in hiring that was built upon month by month, quarter by quarter. By the end of 2016, the economy had seen 75 consecutive months of job growth. So here we are (again): a tight talent market. Over the last year, it has been reported that we have anywhere from 5.5 million to 6.5 million unfilled jobs in the economy today, and every month roughly 3.2-3.3 million full time employees quit their jobs to take a new role in search of something else.[2]

It is definitely a candidate's market for talent. There is a talent shortage predicted to be with us until at least 2050, and companies are looking for ways to find great people and hang on to them.[3] While this may echo the war for talent, things are more complex than they were in the talent market 20 years ago.

Today, we have a multigenerational workforce that will be with us for at least the next 30 years. People want more from work, with work being a place to express their values and make a contribution. They want to work in a way that expresses their beliefs. Technology is changing how we work, where we work, how we connect, our ability to collaborate, and the convergence of work and the rest of our lives.

Values matter, purpose matters, and people want to be valued not just for what they can do but for who they are. Employees want to know that you care about them. Recognition and valuing the individual is important. People want to be developed not only for the job they are in today but also

---

[2] "Business Employment Dynamics Summary," Bureau of Labor Statistics, last modified January 26, 2018, https://www.bls.gov/news.release/cewbd.nr0.htm.
[3] "Demographic 2050 Destiny," The Wall Street Journal, http://graphics.wsj.com/2050-demographic-destiny/.

for the jobs they would like to grow into. The quality of the conversation has changed, employees want real connection that is meaningful. They want to matter and want to trust leaders that value who they are. This is where The Science of Story begins.

Culture is essential in a tough talent market. As you will learn in The Science of Story, working and living with purpose and intention helps you attract and retain great people. Having a compelling story for your employees is just as important as the one you tell your customers. The most important job of leaders is to translate their mission, purpose, vision ,and story for their employees and figure out how to live them every day.

Adam and Hank have offered a way forward in this book for every leader and every organization that aspires to create great results by engaging their people, living their purpose, and telling their story. Consider this a workbook for the soul of your people and your company. It is a field guide on how to create great cultures through developing compelling stories. It offers insight into how to build a culture and organization where people want to join and make a passionate contribution.

I wish you a great journey as you develop and live your story.

Pamela Stroko
Vice-President
HCM Transformation & Thought Leadership
Oracle Corporation
January 2018

Introduction

"The two most important days of a man's life are the day on which he was born and the day on which he discovers why he was born."

—Rev. Ernest T. Campbell

From religions to revolutions, from war to peace, stories are at the heart of human history. And in the last 50 years—particularly in the last 10—stories have become the name of the business marketing game. Budweiser isn't just competing with Amstel Light on taste. They're also competing on answers to questions like: "Where did you come from?" "Where are we going?" "Will you help me become a better global citizen?" Inspire us—or we're drinking Amstel tonight.

Today's fastest-growing companies tell stories that position themselves as agents of change working toward a better future. The cult favorite, fast-casual chain Sweetgreen aims, "To inspire healthier communities by connecting people to real food."[4] Wells Fargo, a well-known financial services company, discusses the following in its value statement, "Regardless of our growing size, scope, and reach, we must never lose sight of putting our customers first and helping them succeed financially."[5]

But, awakening to the power of story as a marketing tool introduces a new temptation: telling stories that aren't exactly, you know, true. In the case of that well-known financial services firm, there was a disconnect between their stated values and their actual values. "Lions hunting zebras" is how the *New York Times* described Wells Fargo's stealthy attack on

---

[4] "Our Story," Sweetgreen, http://www.sweetgreen.com/our-story/.
[5] "Our Firm," Blaustein Clancy Financial Group of Wells Fargo, http://www.blausteinclancy.wfadv.com/Our-Firm.2.htm.

client resources.[6] In October 2016, Wells Fargo became the largest bank ever to lose its accreditation with the Better Business Bureau after aiming to cross-sell eight accounts to every customer, even if that meant giving bad advice or flat-out lying.[7]

The gap between presentation and reality in Wells Fargo's case was extreme, but almost more concerning are the gaps between presentation and reality that exist in many, if not most, companies. And here's the catch: it's not their fault.

Up until recently, companies have succeeded or failed based on profit. The standard for success was simple: make money. But the rules have changed with dizzying speed. We've pivoted from the "greed is good" mentality to "conscious capitalism," a phrase popularized by Whole Foods CEO John Mackey.[8] Businesses that make money by delivering a product or service to their customers at a good value could be undone if their customers decide they're in business for the wrong reasons. They might find their profits start to tank.

And what are the "right reasons" to be in business? Today, the "right" answer aligns with the greater good of humankind. Companies that thrive, "Serve the interests of all major stakeholders—customers, employees, investors, communities, suppliers, and the environment."[9]

Don't panic just because you're confused, or even resentful, of this new expectation that companies give back to society, as well as other key stakeholders. You might be unsure how to remain profitable while running an empathetic, inspiring company. Frankly, the transition from

[6] Stacy Cowley, "'Lions Hunting Zebras': Ex-Wells Fargo Bankers Describe Abuses," *The New York Times*, October 20, 2016, http://www.nytimes.com/2016/10/21/business/dealbook/lions-hunting-zebras-ex-wells-fargo-bankers-describe-abuses.html.

[7] Sylvan Lane, "Wells Fargo loses Better Business Bureau accreditation," *The Hill*, October 20, 2016, http://thehill.com/policy/finance/302080-wells-fargo-loses-better-business-bureau-accreditation.

[8] Kate Lowery, "Conscious Capitalism: A New Book by our Co-Founder and Co-CEO, John Mackey," *Whole Foods Market Blog*, January 11, 2013, http://www.wholefoodsmarket.com/blog/conscious-capitalism-new-book-our-co-founder-and-co-ceo-john-mackey-0.

[9] Jeff King, "Only Conscious Capitalists Will Survive," *Forbes Magazine*, December 4, 2013, https://www.forbes.com/sites/onmarketing/2013/12/04/only-conscious-capitalists-will-survive/.

20th century to 21st century values would induce vertigo in the hardiest of souls. It's no wonder that there's a gap between the stories customers buy and the reality under the hood—the reality of the way companies run, or the story that employees see.

In this book, we'll teach you (as a curious and inspired leader/reader) to thrive as you pursue building a purpose-driven company that does more than blindly and slavishly pursue profit. We'll also teach you to find a story to tell your customers that's true, one that doesn't feel like a charade. In other words, we'll teach you how to put on the same face for your employees that you put on for your customers.

The first step is to identify your purpose—the non-financial, people-first commitment that will guide your strategy, culture, and marketing. We'll also teach you how to passionately explain your company's purpose to the members of your organization so they can fully embrace the concept and contribute at the maximum of their ability. Not only is it easier for leaders to marry their stated purpose with their actions—they must.

Humans are incredibly perceptive creatures. If you're not sincerely excited about what your team is accomplishing together, your employees will know. If you treat your customers like gold, while your employees are treated like second-class citizens (and not properly embraced by purpose so they can believe in and rally around something greater), toxicity will leak into the air, and engagement will live as a concept only, with consequences. Losing employees is expensive. It costs up to 40 percent of an entry-level employee's salary to replace them; 150 percent of a mid-level employee's salary; and 400 percent of a senior employee's salary.[10]

One way for companies to fix the problem of employee engagement is to shop for band-aid treatments. Externally, you could continue to blast and live your brand story through marketing channels and internally share less substantive rhetoric, or take less meaningful actions to enhance the

---

[10] "The Cost of Employee Turnover," *Zen Workplace*, October 28, 2016, www.zenworkplace.com/2014/07/01/cost-employee-turnover/.

employee experience. You wouldn't need our help with that.

There's a better way. You could take the radical step, which we'll describe in detail in this book: stop trying to figure out how to keep employees from leaving and start figuring out how to serve them. Apply the distinctive values you weave through your external storytelling to your internal storytelling, using them as guides to transform your organizational design and culture.

We know that when we hear and see stories on a screen, parts of our brain fires up as if we were participating in the events. We know that stories make the best marketing. What many leaders don't realize is that they're telling a story to their employees every day by the actions they take. That story must manifest not so much in the words they speak, but in their organizational design and the culture they create.

Aaron Dignan, founder of the organizational design firm The Ready, wrote about visiting the headquarters of a Fortune 500 company. He had a gift of a small notebook to deliver to a friend who worked upstairs, and he asked the front desk if he could leave the package with them there. He wrote on *Medium* (the blog-publishing platform) about the exchange that followed:

Them: We do not accept packages of any kind.
Me: Why not?
Them: Because we can't be held responsible for loss or damage.
Me: It's a journal still sealed in the cellophane. What could happen?
Them: It's just policy.
Me: Could I sign something, relinquishing my right to claim any
damages if you lose or damage it in the 30 minutes between now and
when he picks it up? He really needs it.
Them: No.
Me: OMG.

Them: It's just policy.[11]

Your policies tell a story. In this particular story, does the company show it trusts its people? No. Is bureaucracy common sense more important? Take a guess. That's not the kind of story that engages.

In our research for this book, we've dug deep into the science of employee engagement and hit on (or returned to) something most of us have learned in school: Maslow's Hierarchy of Needs. For employees to feel fulfilled and to perform at their best, employers must meet a range of needs, from foundational needs (food, water, safety) to the need for self-actualization. Self-actualization is defined as the realization of one's talents and potentialities. Abraham Maslow said, "Human history is a record of the ways in which human nature has been sold short. The highest possibilities of human nature have practically always been underrated."[12] It is time to change our course and raise the bar so that we can inspire (and achieve) self-actualization in the workplace. It is a journey of many steps.

The first step: To feel fulfilled and to perform at their best, employees need one thing, primarily: a sense of psychological safety, which is defined as, "Being able to show and employ one's self without fear of negative consequences of self-image, status, or career."[13] In other words, employees need to feel sure that they are, and will be, respected and protected.

All the evidence we have accumulated through independent research and over 500 interviews with thought leaders and business executives highlights the fact that you, as an inspired leader, cannot afford to neglect the members of your team. They need to see that you have a genuine commitment not only to them, your product or service, and your clients or customers, but also to the greater community. You need to create an environment in which they can feel they are making a positive contribution

[11] Aaron Dignan. "If the Answer Is 'It's Just Policy,' You're F*cked," *Medium*, November 07, 2015, https://medium.com/the-ready/if-the-answer-is-it-s-just-policy-you-re-fucked-375d1ced3ec2.
[12] Abraham Maslow, *The Farther Reaches of Human Nature* (New York: Penguin Group, 1993), 7.
[13] William Kahn, "Psychological Conditions of Personal Engagement and Disengagement at Work," *Academy of Management Journal* 33, no. 4 (1990): 705.

to the world around them—and be rewarded for it. Purpose transformation is not going to happen if you don't lead by example and take critical and initial actions such as these.

That means to foster this sense of purpose, you have to show your employees the same values you show your customers. You can't tell an authentic and powerful story to the outside world until you are living one inside your company. That's right: you can't fake it. Whatever values you espouse off the record will eventually seep into your company's public persona.

If you wish to move forward, we first suggest you embrace a change in vocabulary. In its strictest sense, "employee" means someone who is hired by someone else and works simply to get paid, i.e., for financial reward. Let's abandon that word. It doesn't fit in a climate where our business focus is purpose-driven. At our company, Mabbly, we talk about our Tribe. The definition of tribe, according to the English Oxford Living Dictionaries, is, "A social division in a traditional society consisting of families or communities linked by social, economic, religious, or blood ties, with a common culture and dialect, typically having a recognized leader."[14]

When people ask why we call ourselves a Tribe at Mabbly, we explain that teams break up and families are dysfunctional, but tribes support one another to survive and thrive, and are united by or share a series of common beliefs. To us, being part of a Tribe speaks of having a relationship and a bond that goes beyond employer-employee. A Tribe, of course, is made up of numerous unique individuals, but the individuals are united in a common culture and for a common cause.

Ultimately, the company can only be as good (in every sense of the word) as its individual members. That's why it's important to never forget that members of your tribe are your principal customers. Your tribe members are your gateway to success. Your tribe members must come

---

[14] *English Oxford Living Dictionaries*, online ed., "tribe."

first. Therefore, you'll find us favoring the use of the word tribe as much as possible throughout this book. You can choose whatever word works best for your company as long as it redefines the employee-employer relationship and defines your company as part of your story.

We're not hopelessly idealistic Millennials. The premise of this book is not something we conjured up in an afternoon brainstorming session—although we are self-confessed "crazy guys on whiteboards" who constantly engage in no-limit, no-holds-barred discussions. Rather, it's a from-the-heart, thoughtful, methodical road map to get you to understand and act on the science of purpose and the science of story, and so much more.

The Science of Story evolved during a two-year odyssey during which we interviewed leaders of more than 500 companies, probing them for the "secret sauce" that made them so successful—companies large and small across a wide spectrum of industries. We included fast-growing start-ups with a vision for a new world and multi-national, publicly traded Goliaths that consistently outperform the market. We looked at the psychology, the research, and the science behind the power of purpose and the power of storytelling. Along the way, we were exhilarated to realize our own sense of mission and purpose: to inspire companies, beginning with the members of their own organization, to make a conscious choice to pursue purpose.

A significant influence for both of us was Simon Sinek's groundbreaking 18-minute TED Talk, the third most-watched talk of all time, and his *New York Times* bestselling book *Start with Why*. He argued that the people and organizations that pause to ask "Why" before they act—and especially before they lead—are more likely to focus on and actually do things that inspire them. They actually tend to be more profitable and influential than others.[15]

We said to each other that starting with "Why" is all well and good,

---

[15] Simon Sinek, *Start With Why: How Great Leaders Inspire Everyone to Take Action* (London: Portfolio/Penguin, 2013).

but how do you discover your "Why" when there are a lot of voices in the room? Five, 50, 500 employees? And even more importantly, how do you, inspired leaders who are influencers and curious readers who desire change, reexamine old habits—needless bureaucracy, unnecessary policies, poor communication—and create a purpose-driven internal culture?

Many companies we interviewed for this book came up with an answer, but the majority did not. Many created a purpose-driven culture, but struggled with implementation: they didn't quite get how to put their Why into effect, not just throughout their company, but also beyond. We had our own ideas—plenty of ideas. But rather than cast them in stone, we decided to test them and, even further, seek out the best of the best. What could we learn from what other businesses were already doing?

When we first started this project, we were a small, rapidly growing digital agency in Chicago's West Loop. We were motivated to build our own company, a lasting enterprise based on purpose, which would forge a stronger bond to our life's work, to the central idea of doing something of real value, while enriching our lives with stronger personal connections. And we instinctively knew that what would work for us would also work for others. We wanted to give back.

So, we set off on a journey of discovery that proved to be more enlightening than we'd ever imagined possible. In researching this book, we interviewed companies that had wholeheartedly embraced the concept of being a purpose-driven organization and others that were tentatively dipping their toes in the water. It was an enthralling, life-altering experience. Their insights have forever enriched us.

On the other side of the coin, we also encountered executives who were cold, unresponsive, skeptical, or even downright hostile. Maybe because the concept of being purpose-driven tugs them out of their comfort zone and out of the creed that they were taught years ago at business school: maximize shareholder value at all costs!

Many organizations knew that the need to discover and implement one's purpose is an essential and fundamental shake-up of the corporate world. But knowing it is no good unless you can communicate and implement it both internally and externally. In our journey, we came to appreciate that those who truly believe their purpose actually tell their story (externally and internally) with conviction. And it dawned on us that we were amassing a treasure trove of dynamic and actionable material that needed to be shared with a wider audience. And just like that, a book was born!

When we had the opportunity to talk with Simon Sinek, he told us, "A 'Why' has to be for others. It's something you give to the world."[16] Specifically, with regard to writing a book, he said it should be motivated by a desire to share what you have learned rather than to obtain fame or fortune: "You have to write a book because you believe (what you have learned) has helped, because you believe it has helped others personally, and you are dying to share this with others because you know it will add value to their lives."[17]

Following that logic, *The Science of Story* is our gift to the world, brought to you in part thanks to the generosity of so many company executives who took the time to share their stories with us.

You could sum up our many, many transcripts by saying, "Brand is a reflection of culture." Nothing is hidden in a reflection. Sure, some companies can temporarily hide toxic elements of their internal culture, but eventually it will bleed into their brand, and the outside world will see it.

To be a brand that has meaning, a brand that transcends profit motive, a brand that has a role in crafting the society of the future, a brand that tells unforgettable stories, you simply have to follow three principles that serve as our mantra:

- Purpose inspires.

---

[16] Simon Sinek (Optimist and Founder of Start With Why) in discussion with the author, July 2015.
[17] Ibid.

- Values guide.

- Habits define.

We'll unpack these galvanizing concepts throughout the pages that follow. Yes, purpose transformation is hard work. But, we've distilled the process into a roadmap that anyone can follow. By the end of this book, you'll be able to set up a process in your organization that will guide you in the years and decades to come.

A few things we need to tell you upfront: when your clear reason for being—your purpose—is applied to your long-term vision and decision-making, the results are earth-shattering. But purpose transformation is not easy. It is not a one-meeting-sort-of-deal. It is not for the faint of heart. And the transformation journey does not have an ultimate destination. As you reach one level of awareness, you will only then realize there is a greater level beyond. Your vision and story will also evolve and expand as you grow. That's what happened to us.

Even though we will repeatedly encourage you to transcend profit motives, it does not mean that we are discounting that business focus. We have discovered that telling your story the right way will yield more fulfilled and productive employees, more loyal and happier customers, and consequently a more sustainable company, which will lead to more personal and financial reward in the end. So we are not taking you down a misguided path.

Chances are that you have opened this book because you are already a champion of purpose. If not, you will be soon enough. Or perhaps you have been lucky enough to have been gifted this book by an existing champion of purpose—in which case you should feel flattered, as they probably see the potential within you. Regardless of why you started reading this book, chances are that you will fight headwinds as you seek to implement our action plan. But the ultimate reward—finding a life's work—will be transformative for you and your organization.

On the face of it, this book is for more senior-level leaders who are in a position to affect major change, but if you're a manager or an employee who wants to make change happen in your organization, you'll learn how to speak clearly and confidently to get buy-in from up-top for a purpose transformation.

But first, let's share with you the stories of our personal journeys before we lead you on find your own.

Meet Adam

I never thought I would write a book. Never. I immigrated as a young adolescent to the U.S. in 1989 with my parents. My first experience of life in my new homeland was to see my dad, who had been a lead musician in Belarus, part of the former Soviet Union, become a dishwasher and my mom, an experienced engineer, get a job in data entry.

Back then, the family focus was simple: survival. My choice of education was dictated by where I could make the most money and find my gig tolerable. I love movies, and around that time, the movie *Wall Street* had been a smash hit. The memorable line "Greed is good" epitomized the life and swagger of the high-rolling, sharply dressed investment bankers in the film. They seemed to have it all. Sign me up. I was ready to join the ranks.

I got my Master's degree in Finance. I was crazy enough to think that financial derivatives were going to be my gig. I cast aside the numerous exciting attempts at being an entrepreneur that I'd made before graduation, and embraced a new attitude: enough having fun! Now is the time for real work. I embarked on a career in corporate finance.

Four years later, I had to admit that course was definitely not for me. So, I switched career paths to real estate. People were making serious money there. I wore different hats: property developer, owner of a mortgage company, partner in a general contracting company. I even found myself getting a masonry license. All in all, I contributed to what became the great recession of 2007. My reward: complete financial ruin. After five years in the business, I found myself waking up in the morning with stress-induced bruises on my body and flashes across my forehead. (Nope, Lord Voldemort was not coming.)

In 2007, I entered entrepreneurship and thought, "Wow, can I really begin to enjoy what I do?" After a number of failures (but amazing experiences, earning a Master's degree in start-ups in the process), I found myself with three kids and a digital agency—Mabbly. My business partner and co-author, Hank, and I knew that we were going to build a company where we would want to work, where we would wake up and feel inspired day in and day out. Our attitude was that no matter what happened—we would figure it out. Our mantra was and still is, "two guys in a canoe." That was how we signaled to each other that we would survive and thrive even if we were just two guys in a canoe floating down the Chicago River. Our backgrounds and styles are completely different—almost opposites—but we are united by some clear principles and values: giving all of ourselves, disrupting the status quo, and a driving passion to inspire others.

When we started to research and write this book, it changed my life. The interviews and discussions with leaders of companies across industries and markets have opened my eyes to the simple conclusion: I can give myself permission to do what I love. Perhaps it's not the most brilliant observation ever made, but it rocked my world.

This book, this journey, is an expression and evolution of my beliefs. The world can do better than waste human potential on being miserable at work and perpetuating the cycle of the "working zombies." Now is the time to take the next step in the evolution of work. I want to help drive that transformation forward with my life's work.

Meet Hank

I was born in Cincinnati, Ohio just across the river from Northern Kentucky, and when I get talking after a couple of beers, a bit of a twang comes out to prove it. My journey in life has been simple, growing up a son of purposeful people who dedicated their lives to others. My parents' careers revolved around serving people through social work, non-profits, and pediatric oncology. They taught me that the measure of success is the distance between what you give and what you take from relationships.

But this didn't sink in right away. I was a rebellious youngster struggling with demons of inadequacy. As a kid, I slept on the cafeteria tables of the University of Cincinnati's graduate schools while my mom finished her nursing education. It was a gritty existence. Still today, I can picture my young mom crying in the car because they wouldn't let her on the PTA. Then I think of her, during my younger brother's school years, becoming the PTA president. My mom has been a source of enduring positivity in my life and the person I most admire.

I went to good schools with wealth around me. Not appreciating my parents' level of intellectual success, I didn't understand why the children of major executives at P&G and GE got new BMWs at the age of 16, while I got to help fix up our old house or volunteer for whatever our mom signed us up to do each weekend. My foundation in life was raw, real, and mostly built upon merit.

My upbringing gave me a sense of purpose, but there was always a strength, hunger, and dedication inside me to succeed and to be "rich"— financially rich. As I developed in my formative years, I was drawn to the "rich guy" mentality. Movies from the turn of the millennium influenced my vision of a professional career. One specific scene comes to mind in the film *Boiler Room*, starring Ben Affleck, in which he throws his Ferrari keys on the table and delivers the most inspiring speech to any young ego:

So, now you know what's possible. Let me tell you what's required. You are required to work your f***ing a** off at this firm. We want winners here, not pikers. A piker walks at the bell. A piker asks how much vacation you get in the first year. Vacation? People come and work at this firm for one reason: to become filthy rich. We're not here to make friends. We're not savin' the manatees, guys. You want vacation time? Go teach third grade, public school.[18]

So, when I started applying myself, many unique and worldly experiences came my way. During my early career with a major enterprise, I enjoyed frequent overseas travel. I even got to live in Australia and India. I was driven by the idea that I was going to win and take care of everyone around me. Becoming financially rich, and bound by nothing, drove every decision. It gave me purpose, identity, and focus, or so I thought. I was on track for what I had envisioned as success.

During my late twenties, when my best friends made a mass exodus from major corporate enterprises into startups, I found myself wanting. My roommate, for instance, launched Uber Chicago from our apartment, and other friends seemed to be involved in every hip startup in town. I wanted in and embarked on the typical entrepreneurial journey of ups and downs—until Mabbly. I finally realized that knowing one's true purpose overruled everything else. They say partnerships are like marriages— you realize why it never worked out with anyone else until you meet the right person. Adam is that right person for me. He is one of the most important relationships in my life. Our ability to complement each other and communicate efficiently is beyond fulfilling and rewarding. It's been a pleasure to embark on this journey with my business partner, co-author, and friend, Adam. Welcome to *The Science of Story*.

Our Journey

Where are we going in this book? First, we will introduce you to the science behind the power of purpose and the power of storytelling. Then we'll walk you through the plan we've devised to unveil purpose to your organization and motivate your people to wholeheartedly embrace this far-sighted approach. Throughout the book and in the "They Live It" case

---

[18] Ben Younger, *Boiler Room*, DVD, directed by Ben Younger (2000; New York: New Line Cinema & Team Todd, 2000), DVD.

studies at the end, you'll meet individuals and organizations that have been on the journey themselves. Finally, we will introduce you to our research platform called ProHabits, a way to discover daily habits that build enlightened cultures that value "being" as much as "doing."

We intend this to be an epic journey of transformation for you and your organization. You will be inspired, and when you are inspired—truly gut-fired-up-can't-sleep inspired—transformation happens.

Starve the Ego, Feed the Soul

There's a story we like—reportedly, an ancient Native American proverb, that goes like this:

One evening an old Cherokee told his grandson about a battle that goes on inside people. He said, "My son, the battle is between two 'wolves' inside us all. One is Evil. It is anger, envy, jealousy, sorrow, regret, greed, arrogance, self-pity, guilt, resentment, inferiority, lies, false pride, superiority, and ego. The other is Good. It is joy, peace, love, hope, serenity, humility, kindness, benevolence, empathy, generosity, truth, compassion and faith."

The grandson thought about it for a minute and then asked his grandfather: "Which wolf wins?"

The old Cherokee simply replied, "The one you feed."[19]

In simple terms, it's up to you. Which "wolf" do you want to feed? Good or evil? Positive or negative? Do you want a life and a business with purpose or one that's meaningless? Do you want your tribe to be committed and fulfilled, to know that they are genuine partners in your enterprise with shared beliefs and goals?

It is time to make a conscious choice about which wolf to feed. We hope you make the right choice, and move on with us to discover how to

---

[19] Debbie Hampton, "The Wolves Within," *The Best Brain Possible*, September 8, 2014, https://www.thebestbrainpossible.com/the-wolves-within/.

seamlessly merge your company's outward story about what you do and who you are with your internal story and how to build a brand that truly reflects your culture.

CHAPTER 1
The Science of Purpose

"Carve your name on hearts, not tombstones. A legacy is etched into the minds of others and the stories they share about you."

—*Shannon L. Alder, Inspirational Author*

There's a famous story about President John F. Kennedy's first visit to the NASA headquarters in 1962. Touring the facility with his entourage, the President encountered a broom-wielding janitor. Ignoring the assembled dignitaries, he stopped for a chat and asked the janitor exactly what he did at NASA. The response: "Sir, I'm helping put a man on the moon."[20]

Here was a man who had one of the most unglamorous jobs at the space agency, but he felt passionately involved and connected to its purpose and to fulfilling the ambitious mission announced by Kennedy the year before. The janitor felt he was part of something that was far greater than any individual.

It's an instructive story (even if it may be apocryphal) and one that every corporate leader should consider because it begs the questions:

- How would every member of *your* organization answer the question of "what do you do here"?

- What do *they* feel about their role in achieving your company's vision?

- Are *you* truly living the kind of corporate culture you espouse?

In this chapter, we'll look at the behavioral science behind purpose,

---

[20] Laura Eurich, "Pick Purpose, Not Passion," *Colorado Springs Independent*, May 1, 2013, https://www.csindy.com/coloradosprings/pick-purpose-not-passion/Content?oid=2666903.

which drives motivation, health, and performance, along with several theories of organizational psychology. But first, we need to talk about the science that *doesn't* apply to business anymore.

As a quick aside, we recognize that to some, purpose might sound a lot like vision. Before we go on, let's make a critical distinction. In our journey, we have encountered many references to mission statements and vision statements. However, leaders often had a difficult time recalling those perfectly curated statements. That's because those words tended to be static versus dynamic. In fact, not until we encountered purpose-driven organizations did we experience how the clarity of having purpose truly inspired passion and drive. That's why vision and mission doesn't quite equate to purpose. So, if you don't yet have the latter, please push on.

Survival of the Kindest—
How Business Has Changed

The 1987 movie *Wall Street* glamorized the financial hustlers who did whatever it took to claw their way to the top, trampling anyone who got in their way. Gordon Gekko's character, played by Michael Douglas, makes the famous "greed is good" speech.[21] It spoke to the times. It was a celebration, in a way, of the "survival of the fittest" mindset.

That phrase, often attributed to Charles Darwin, was actually coined several years before *On the Origin of Species* came out—and it was used to describe the way an ideal economy would function, not natural selection. British philosopher Herbert Spencer was arguing for laissez-faire capitalism, an economic system where businesses could compete with each other as ruthlessly as they liked without government intervention into—among other things—employee conditions.[22]

---

[21] Francesco Guerrera, "How 'Wall Street' changed Wall Street," *Financial Times*, September 24, 2010, https://www.ft.com/content/7e55442a-c76a-11df-aeb1-00144feab49a.
[22] Andrew Costly, "Bill of Rights in Action," *Constitutional Rights Foundation*, Spring 2003, accessed November 28, 2017, http://www.crf-usa.org/bill-of-rights-in-action/bria-19-2-b-social-darwinism-and-american-laissez-faire-capitalism.html.

Spencer had an impact on how Americans came to believe businesses should function. He even affected the U.S. Supreme Court's interpretation of the Constitution. In 1905, after the Court struck down a law trying to limit the workweek of bakers to 60 hours, Justice Oliver Wendell Holmes lamented the influence of the "survival of the fittest" mentality: "The 14th Amendment does not enact Mr. Herbert Spencer's *Social Statics*."[23]

Spencer, Darwin, what does it matter—they both knew what they were talking about. Right? Not so fast, says Christopher L. Kukk, PhD, Professor of Political Science and Social Science at Western Connecticut State University. The well-known (and well-worn) expression, he says, has been widely misrepresented and, on the contrary, one of Darwin's key conclusions was that humanity's success hinges more on its level of compassion than anything else.[24]

According to Kukk, the work of Darwin, and others, shows the evolution of society increasingly favors approaches to human interaction that are "compassionate and cooperative over callous and competitive." Compassionate and cooperative. Not callous and competitive. Survival of the *kindest*. Not survival of the fittest.

Kukk, author of *The Compassionate Achiever: How Helping Others Fuels Success*, says, "Selfish people and even bullies may win a couple of rounds or sets in the game of life, but they rarely win the match or game; it is the compassionate people who win."[25]

And it's increasingly becoming more expedient to think of business as an opportunity to serve. Aaron Hurst, co-founder of Imperative, the career development technology platform and author of *The Purpose Economy*, asserts a series of shifts are happening in our economy led by Millennials shunning conventional careers in favor of creating community-oriented

---

[23] Ibid.

[24] Christopher Kukk, "Survival of the Fittest Has Evolved: Try Survival of the Kindest," *NBCNews. com*, March 8, 2017, https://www.nbcnews.com/better/relationships/survival-fittest-has-evolved-try-survival-kindest-n730196.

[25] Christopher Kukk, *The Compassionate Achiever* (New York, NY: HarperOne, 2017).

businesses.[26] It's a generation that shares everything from cars to rooms and in an economy that gives people and society a purpose, an opportunity to be part of something bigger than themselves. Says Hurst, "The Information Economy radically reshaped every industry and corner of society. A new economic era is now emerging that again is reshaping everything from what we buy to how we work. Those cities, organizations and leaders who embrace it will be the ones that thrive in this exciting next chapter."[27]

In other words, this book is not a touchy-feely endeavor. Far from it. We're endorsing feeling good while doing good *and* making a good profit at the same time.

Let's start with feeling good. Why does it feel so good to have purpose? Why is it one of the biggest factors behind happiness in the 21st century? We will now explore the importance of purpose and its effects on individuals and companies.

Individuals and Purpose

According to an analysis of data collected from 6,000 participants by researchers Patrick L. Hill of Carleton University and Nicholas A. Turiano of West Virginia University, you're more likely to become more financially successful than your peers if you're someone with a sense of purpose.[28]

The Imperative-New York University study mentioned earlier found that that knowing your purpose makes you 50 percent more likely to have meaningful relationships at work, and 54 percent more likely to feel your work has a positive impact. It also recorded that purpose-oriented individuals have a 64 percent higher level of career fulfillment and remain with a company 20 percent longer.[29]

---

[26] Aaron Hurst, *The Purpose Economy* (Boise, ID: Elevate, a Russell Media company, 2014).

[24] Ibid.

[28] "A Meaningful Job Linked to Higher Income and a Longer Life," *Association for Psychological Science*, January 3, 2017, https://www.psychologicalscience.org/news/minds-business/a-meaningful-job-linked-to-higher-income-and-a-longer-life.html.

[29] "2015 Workforce Purpose Index," *Imperative*, 2015, accessed November 28, 2017, https://cdn.imperative.com/media/public/Purpose_Index_2015.

But—perhaps ironically—for the happiest and most fulfilled individuals, raking in more cash is way down on their list of priorities. We know this from a number of studies, including one spearheaded by the think tank, The Happiness Research Institute, which probed the lives of 2,500 people in Denmark, a country whose people top just about every barometer of happiness, including job satisfaction. According to Eurobarometer 2014, 94 percent of Danish employees are satisfied with their conditions at work, whereas the average in the European Union is 77 percent. The number one factor affecting job satisfaction by far was having a sense of purpose. It has a greater influence than salary, results, and relationships with colleagues combined.[30]

Cecilie Eriksen, a Ph.D., from Aarhus University in Denmark says, "Historically, the reason to go to work has, to a large extent, been exclusively to feed your family. For many people nowadays, work is much more than that. We work because we feel that it matters—both to society and to who we are."[31]

Pulitzer Prize-winning author and historian Studs Terkel crisscrossed the United States in the early 1970s interviewing people for his book *Working: People Talk About What They Do All Day and How They Feel About What They Do*. He spoke at length with more than a hundred people whose occupations ranged from gravediggers to studio heads.

His conclusion: "Work is about a search for daily meaning as well as daily bread, for recognition as well as cash, for astonishment rather than torpor; in short, for a sort of life, rather than a Monday to Friday sort of dying." In effect, he was eloquently making a case for the value of a sense of purpose, especially when, as he put it, many people "have jobs that are

---

[30] "Danish Employees Are the Happiest in the EU," *Copenhagen Capacity*, May 5, 2014, http://www.copcap.com/newslist/2014/danish-employees-are-the-happiest-in-the-eu.
[31] "What is the point?," Soft Skills Learning, http://softskillslearning.ie/existential-purpose-meaning-philosophy/.

too small for our spirit."[32]

Purpose, in fact, transcends everything. One of the best examples of all is Viktor Frankl, Austrian neurologist, psychiatrist, and Holocaust survivor. His best-selling book *Man's Search for Meaning* chronicles his years in Nazi concentration camps and emphasizes the importance of finding meaning in all forms of existence, even under the most brutal and inhumane conditions. Frankl became one of the key figures in existential therapy and a prominent source of inspiration for humanistic psychologists.

Frankl maintained that man's search for meaning is a *primary* force in life and not a "secondary rationalization." In other words, it's a fundamental underpinning of life itself rather than an attempt to find logical reasons to explain one's sense of being, or one's sense of purpose. He wrote, "Man… is able to live and even to die for the sake of his ideals and values."[33]

Of course, individuals must create their own sense of meaning. Corporate leadership can't fabricate it for them. However, you can create supportive environments that foster opportunities to produce meaning. You can find ways to enable employees to understand and appreciate the impact of their contribution and to recognize that their being engaged matters. It can come from connecting the dots between their role and what they do to the ultimate success of the company, whether that connection is a direct or indirect one. It can also come from recognition: acknowledging the results that they achieve make a difference in the big picture. And incidentally, recognition doesn't need to be grandiose or even monetary. It can take the form of something as simple as a short handwritten thank you note or a positive call-out at a staff meeting.

Note: It's an Uphill Road for Some

Sometimes elements of your upbringing slow the process of finding

---

[32] Studs Terkel, *Working: People Talk About What They Do All Day and How They Feel About What They Do* (New York/London: The New Press, 1997).

[33] Viktor Frankl, *Man's Search for Meaning* (Boston: Beacon Press, 2006).

your individual purpose. Take Gena Chigrinov, the CFO of Mabbly. He says of his home country, Ukraine, "I'm coming from a world where dollars are the only thing people care about." That's partially because a big chunk of the population there lives in absolute poverty. The average worker's monthly salary is below $300.

"The way that we do business, the way we work, and the way I grew up was oriented toward the bottom line. The only purpose people cared about was how to get rich. Some people can go to the extreme of murder. Some people steal money from the budget. And so on and so forth."

Gena moved to the UK when he was 16. At first, his value system didn't change much. He was studying finance and economics. "It was dollar-oriented, and nobody teaches purpose in school." He was planning on becoming an investment banker. But when he realized he'd have to work 24/7, and that he'd have to constantly be doing presentations for a company that he didn't completely understand the workings of, he felt shortchanged. He'd seen his dad logging long hours for decades and didn't want to follow that path.

Gena's shift in perspective toward living with purpose has been incremental. First he realized that if he was going to work 24/7, he at least wanted to build something of his own, or have a big impact on a small team. Observing teams of purpose-oriented people started to slowly chip away at the bottom-line mentality he grew up with. "My mind has changed billions of times in the past four years." His personal purpose, now, is to deliver value to everyone he works with, even to the people he doesn't naturally click with.[34]

Surprisingly, those who have to undo foundational beliefs about profit coming before everything often become some of the most passionate spokespeople for purpose you'll find.

---

[34] Gennadiy (Gena) (CFO at Mabbly) in communication with the author, 2016-2017.

The Health Advantage

People with a sense of purpose even live longer, Hill and Turiano discovered. Hill says, "Our findings point to the fact that finding a direction in life, and setting overarching goals for what you want to achieve, can help you actually live longer...there's something unique about finding a purpose that seems to be leading to greater longevity."[35]

Purpose—engagement and working toward goals as we age—is a crucially positive factor for vitality, productivity, and lower rates of cognitive decline, stroke, and heart attack. Other research shows a 42 percent increase in contentment and a 31 percent increase in the intensity of love in a romantic relationship.[36]

As Richard J. Leider, author of *The Power of Purpose: Find Meaning, Live Longer, Better*, says, "All people seem to have a natural desire and capacity to contribute somehow to life. Each of us wants to leave footprints. And each of us has a unique purpose. Having a reason to get up in the morning is associated in numerous scientific studies with better mental and physical health and greater longevity. Purpose can add not only years to your life, but life to your years."[37]

Consumers and Purpose

We've known for some time that consumers want to shop ethically. Research documents this phenomenon: 92 percent of Millennials are more likely to purchase goods and services from ethical companies;[38] 56 percent of U.S. consumers cease to buy from companies they believe are unethical

---

[35] "A Meaningful Job Linked to Higher Income and a Longer Life," *Association for Psychological Science*, January 3, 2017, https://www.psychologicalscience.org/news/minds-business/a-meaningful-job-linked-to-higher-income-and-a-longer-life.html#.WRbt_2jyvlU.

[36] "What Scientific Studies Show Purpose Gives You," Purpose Guides Institute, https://www.purposeguides.org/what-scientific-studies-show-purpose-gives-you/#.

[37] Richard Leider, *The Power of Purpose* (Oakland, CA: Berrett-Koehler Publishers, Inc., 2015).

[38] "Aflac Corporate Social Responsibility Survey Fact Sheet," Aflac, last modified November 16, 2015, https://www.philanthropy.com/items/biz/pdf/AflacCorporateSocialResponsibility.pdf.

and 35 percent will do so even if there's no substitute available.[39]

While behaving ethically doesn't always amount to having a clear purpose, it's the first step on that journey. And purpose-driven companies are more likely to thrive in terms of brand perception and financial results:

- 40 percent of a company's reputation is determined by its purpose (the other 60 percent depending on its performance).[40]

- Purpose-led companies outperformed the S&P 500 10x between 1996 and 2011.[41]

- A strong, well-communicated purpose can contribute as much as 17 percent improvement in financial performance.[42]

Consumers are increasingly making buying decisions based on purpose. You see it in the growing number of people buying shoes from Toms or eyeglasses from Warby Parker. Consumers are choosing to shop at companies that provide support and benefits to those who are less fortunate. You see it with companies opening their business to the public gaze—being transparent in ways that would seem shocking to big business just a few years ago.

Take the clothing manufacturer, Everlane, for example. It calls its business practice "Radical Transparency," and says, "We believe our customers have a right to know how much their clothes cost to make."[43] To that end, Everlane reveals the true costs behind all of its products—from materials to labor to transportation. It then sells them to its customers for less than the traditional retail markup. And the company makes a strong

---

[39] Lauren Bonetto, "56 Percent of Americans Stop Buying from Brands They Believe Are Unethical," *Mintel*, November 18, 2015, http://www.mintel.com/press-centre/social-and-lifestyle/56-of-americans-stop-buying-from-brands-they-believe-are-unethical.

[40] Ibid.

[41] Rajendra Sisodia, David Wolfe, and Jagdish N. Sheth, *Firms of Endearment: How World-Class Companies Profit from Passion and Purpose* (Upper Saddle River, NJ: Pearson Education, 2007).

[42] "Latest News: Leading Corporations Believe in Corporate Purpose, according to the Burson-Marsteller/IMD Power of Purpose Study," *Burson Marsteller*, September 2, 2013, http://www.burson-marsteller.eu/latest-news/leading-corporations-believe-in-corporate-purpose-according-to-the-burson-marstellerimd-power-of-purpose-study/.

[43] "About," Everlane, https://www.everlane.com/about.

point of only partnering with the best ethical companies around the world. Everlane communicates that message extremely effectively, highlighting the fact that stories deliver the essential human connection, beyond the typical recitation of facts and figures that many corporate leaders feel are indispensable.

It's important to note that it's never too late for a company to break from a profit-first mindset and pursue purpose. Some organizations may only turn to their purpose transformation because nothing else is working and buy into the mindset more soulfully later on. These late-comers richly benefit, as well.

Take Louisville Slugger for instance. It's one of those brands that everyone knows—a brand unrivaled in the history of Major League Baseball. More than 100 million bats have been crafted since the very first one back in 1884 and over 60 percent of players in the Baseball Hall of Fame have played with a Louisville Slugger.[44] Even today, the brand continues to dominate the game in both wood and aluminum bat categories with players across the Major League, as well as countless other players on semi-pro and recreational teams.

When the company's winning streak began to decline, however, senior executives, led by John Hillerich IV, a descendent of the company's founder, decided it was time to reinvigorate the brand and the business. In 2012, the company discovered and developed its purpose as part of an overall corporate reinvention, ultimately leading to a brand relaunch in 2013 and the acquisition by Wilson Sporting Goods in 2015.

Kyle Schlegel, currently the Global Marketing Director of Racquet Sports at Wilson, had previously served as the Global Vice President of Marketing at Hillerich & Bradsby Co., Louisville Slugger's former parent company. He told us that the mixture of existing leadership and new leaders wanted to lay a foundation that would carry the brand for the next

---

[44] "Our History," Louisville Slugger, http://www.slugger.com/en-us/our-history.

130 years. As the team reflected on the things that had made Louisville Slugger successful, it was evident that it was all about doing what was right for the player and helping him or her to achieve their dreams. This thinking and a great deal of discussion ultimately led to the statement: "Making players great."

One thing that helped make the discovery process (a key step of the purpose journey covered more fully in Chapter 3) and the new foundation crystal clear was the existence of the Louisville Slugger Museum, one of the top sports destinations in the country. The "purpose team" often found themselves roaming the museum, looking for inspiration and anecdotes that would help bring the brand story to life.

Kyle adds, "As we 'sat with' this new purpose and looked at all the ways it could inform the company, it became clear that 'players' was a much more far-reaching thought than just the athletes on the field. This spoke to our own employees, our retailers, the patrons at the museum, and anyone else that touched the Louisville Slugger brand. They are all players and this became incredibly inspiring!"

He says that stretching their thinking regarding "players" led to a new way of engaging their retailers: "We shifted from an 'us versus them' mentality to one of partnership. What was good for the retailer and helped them to succeed was also good for Louisville Slugger. We shifted to starting every retailer meeting by asking them what they were trying to achieve, the challenges they faced, and how they were going about taking on those challenges. This allowed our team to truly listen and understand and, in sharing our thoughts and plans, our thought process began to truly reflect 'making them great.' We saw this quickly affect our relationships in a positive manner and what was once an 'us versus them' became a 'we' as we strived for mutually beneficial programs."

The new company purpose became ingrained in everything the company did and served as a touchstone during all critical moments in the years to follow. None proved more critical than the acquisition by Wilson followed by a surge in sales, a move that has taken Louisville Slugger from the #4 bat brand to #1 again for the first time in more than a decade.

Kyle shares, "Working at Louisville Slugger was a once-in-a-lifetime experience where we could truly see the purpose come to life in all that we stood for and all that we did. It's 'easy' to come up with a brand purpose statement. At Louisville Slugger, I felt that we truly lived it out."

Historical company events reflect that inspirational purpose. Louisville Slugger was right there with Jackie Robinson when he broke the color barrier. Also, it was the first brand in history to sign an athlete as an endorser.

Kyle says, "This pioneering spirit is still part of the brand today and I'm confident we will see many more breakthroughs in the future. The brand's purpose empowers those that work on the brand to look beyond the playing field, as well for where those breakthroughs might come."[45]

Having said that, in recent years, Louisville Slugger has already broadened its focus far beyond bats while still remaining true to its "making them great" purpose. It has achieved greater success through piloting innovations in performance technology by creating fielding and batting gloves, helmets, catcher's gear, equipment bags, training aids, and accessories. It now sells performance equipment for baseball and softball for all ages and all skill levels, from someone stepping on to the diamond for the first time to the greatest pros in the history of the game.

No longer is business a means to an end or an engine of profit for a select few. Business is much more than that: business is now defined by its purpose. And capitalism is only going to get more conscious. A recent PwC report shows CEOs expect that the demand for purpose in business will increase nearly 300 percent by 2020.[46] That's why we make the case

---

[45] Kyle Schlegel (Global Marketing Director of Racquet Sports at Wilson) in discussion with the author, February 2017.
[46] "20 Years inside the Mind of the CEO...What's Next?" *PwC*, 2017, accessed November 28, 2017, https://www.pwc.com/gx/en/ceo-survey/2017/pwc-ceo-20th-survey-report-2017.pdf.

that it is compassionate people who ultimately win in business.

"What happens if you don't believe us?"

One company became a Mabbly client after losing a major opportunity—doing business with Starbucks. When they met with the Starbucks decision-makers, they launched into their standard sales and promotional pitch. You know the kind of thing: "We're a $100-million company…we have over 100 years of experience and a proven management team…our services include x, y, z…we always deliver on time…blah, blah, blah." But they were stopped dead in their tracks when the Starbucks team interrupted and said, "That's not what we asked. What we want to know is what you believe in as an organization. What is your culture like? Why do you exist as an organization?"

Unfortunately, our newly acquired client didn't have a purpose-focused brand story at that time. Taken aback, the senior executives of this major firm scrambled to come up with an answer. Purpose? Beliefs? Culture? What's all that got to do with business? Starbucks abruptly stopped the conversation. It was not a fit for them. They made it clear that they only work with companies whose culture aligns with theirs and are grounded in purpose that is internally and externally shared.

Just a little research would have educated our new client to the fact that Starbucks is much more than a purveyor of coffee. Upfront on the Starbucks website you'll find the statement:

To say Starbucks purchases and roasts high-quality whole bean coffees is very true. That's the essence of what we do—but it hardly tells the whole story. Every day, we go to work hoping to do two things: share great coffee with our friends and help make the world a little better. It was true when the first Starbucks opened in 1971, and it's just as true today.[47]

---

[47] "Company Information," Starbucks, https://www.starbucks.com/about-us/company-information.

Starbucks knows what it believes. The company, therefore, only wants to work with other companies that know what they believe in, and with people who share those beliefs.

In the rest of this book, we'll show you how to discover and define what you believe in, and how to extend that purpose to your corporate values, strategy, and culture.

CHAPTER 2
The Journey

"But beware of looking for goals: look for a way of life. Decide how you want to live and then see what you can do to make a living within that way of life. But you say, 'I don't know where to look; I don't know what to look for.'"

—Hunter S. Thompson, American Journalist

The journey to becoming a genuinely purpose-driven company that appreciates how to instill values in its tribe is not for the faint of heart. It's a journey with an ultimate destination that brings the kind of fulfillment most people have only dreamed about. It's life-changing and transformational, both for the organization and the individuals who comprise the company. Sometimes this journey has moments that really rock you.

An innocent question from his young daughter changed everything for Steven DuPuis, head of the innovation and design group that bears his name, the DuPuis Group. Steven's major clients, for whom he delivered branding solutions, innovation, and growth opportunities, were big processed food companies. Ironically, his family only ate healthy foods. His wake-up call came one day 10 years ago when his eight-year-old daughter asked, "Why can't I eat any of the stuff you work on?"

It hit Steven like a sledgehammer. He told us, "I realized I was living two lives. One where my wife, a major health-food advocate, fed the family organic, nutritious food at home, and the other where I was building a business through marketing and designing products that were less-than-good for you."

That set him off on a drive to shift his purpose: to practice in business what he believed in his personal life. It was a complete 180-degree shift in the DuPuis Group. It was a realization that allowed Steven to alter his focus and steer the efforts of the DuPuis Group toward changing the food system and bringing healthy foods to the masses. It was a way to live and practice what he believed in.

At the time, the DuPuis Group was particularly known for its expertise in the marketing of kids' brands—everything from Pop-Tarts to Fruit Roll-Ups to all kinds of sugary drinks. It was time to pursue and promote change: "We had created an economic engine that supported lots of people, so I set out to make the change by using our knowledge of marketing strategies that targeted kids to effect positive change."

This resulted in the DuPuis Group being hired by the New York Attorney General as expert marketers to prove R.J. Reynolds was using flavored cigarettes to get children hooked on smoking. New York won this effort and the cigarettes were removed from the market. Furthermore, DuPuis became a respected voice in the crusade against the rising obesity rate in children and its connection to the foods they were eating. Steven promoted the responsibility of the food industry to provide nutritious foods for kids rather than sugar-laden products. It wasn't easy, and there was plenty of denial and resistance, not to mention loss of business for the Group.

To prove and build authenticity, the DuPuis Group got involved with nonprofits. It provided its services pro bono to display commitment to helping create a food system that is good for both people and our planet and to gain knowledge, as well. Steven became a founding member of the Wildlife Friendly Enterprise Network, which focuses on "Building Economies to Save Ecologies." The DuPuis Group also worked with the National Audubon Society in developing a certification program for food products that would save birds and restore grasslands. This led to their work with the National Tropical Botanical Garden to develop a market and supply chain for breadfruit products, a forgotten superfood.

Ultimately, these desperate yet symbiotic efforts have paid off. Some of the big food companies Steven's team used to work with are returning to the DuPuis Group to get help in realigning and creating healthy, responsible products.

How important is the company's "Why?" Says Steven, "Over the past few years, I have seen our group embrace a new energy and passion for the work we do. Our clients sense this and are drawn to having us take on new challenges for them. Because we are aware of our 'Why' and its aspirations, we are more conscious of our results. Big or small, we notice them and celebrate them."

To create impact *in* the system, he says, takes time and patience and comes through small steps. Recently, they worked with Campbell Soup Company to develop disruptive business models that have guided the food giant in new product innovation and influenced M&A activity focused on organic, local, and non-GMO initiatives.

Steven reminds us, "My daughter made me question my purpose." To survive and thrive in business and life we need to continually challenge our purpose and question its meaning and relevance in all we do.[48]

But you can't embark on any journey without knowing how you're going to get there. You need an overall strategy that is logical, doable, and motivational; a road map that gets you to your goal; a road map that gives you the opportunity to drive forward at your own pace and via the route that makes the most sense for you and your Tribe. For some organizations, pushing along at freeway speed is the no-nonsense, fastest, and most direct approach. For other organizations, the route might be a little slower and a little more circuitous.

In our own business journey, and our journey in writing this book, we have identified stages that lead to the creation and development of a thriving purpose-driven organization. Each stage has its own unique properties, challenges, demands, and solutions. As we ready to introduce

---

[48] Steven DuPuis (Founder of DuPuis Group) in discussion with the author, July 2016.

them, it's a good time for another critical call-out to help determine if this journey is for you. Here's the challenge: If the majority of the leadership doesn't align around the idea of defining and communicating what you believe in (what we are calling purpose) versus what you do, stop…at least for now. This core idea will guide every subsequent stage in the process and without this collective understanding, this journey will not be beneficial. So, if you are still onboard (and we hope you are), let's move on with a high-level overview of the stages, which we probe and unpack in the chapters to come.

Believe

The first stage, and the one that we've unofficially been writing about thus far, is Believe. To sum it up, if you are open-minded enough to accept the need to find a purpose to believe in, you have already passed through this stage. In terms of what's to come, we can't claim it's going to be easy. It's absolutely *not* going to be easy, but we can promise you it will be transforming. You will see that a personal journey to find purpose translates into professional purpose and the finding of "a life's work." You will no longer "work to live." What's more, you will help others share in these same transformational rewards. There is great merit and value in being the agent of change—and that's you. So let's go on together and move forward to the next stage: Discover.

Discover

Let's be clear, discovering your purpose is not a matter of conjuring up a catchy, feel-good tagline. We've lost count of the number of times Chief Marketing Officers have proudly trotted out their latest snazzy slogan as the embodiment of their corporate being. We've heard too many charismatic, smooth-talking CEOs pontificating about their goal of, "Establishing long-lasting relationships." Really? That's what we call "Cliché Armageddon." What most of them are saying, in reality is, that they want the dollar value that a long-term, repeat customer brings. But they haven't thought beyond the bottom line. Purposeful corporate leaders think beyond the bottom line and understand the far-flung human ramifications of every decision and interaction. That's a major shift.

The Discover stage is when you put together a team of "Inspired Purpose Champions" (IPC) to lead the overall effort. We'll get into the details of exactly how that works in Chapter Three on the Discover process. In short, the IPC team seeks input from all levels of an organization, challenging individuals to have the courage to rise above the easy, ingrained clichés and the demands of sales cycles. The IPC team becomes the beating heart of the organization until what we describe as a "Purpose Thesis" is developed.

The hardest part of the Discover stage is getting started and getting the conversation going. During your in-house strategy sessions, you need to start talking in terms of purpose and meaning instead of sales initiatives and operational efficiencies. We like to call these sessions Purpose Jams. They are no-holds-barred, free-thinking, brainstorming events that construct the Purpose Thesis. Participants from throughout the organization have an equal say and nothing is off limits. At first, it can be intimidating and alarming, but it becomes enlightening as, hopefully, the strong link between the individual's reason for being and the organization's reason for being become apparent. It is a journey of awakening.

For some, a personal transformation is realized. We call it "Getting wind under your wings." For others, there will be a disconnect and perhaps a realization that they are not in harmony with the organization and its newfound purpose. But that's OK, too. It may be time for them to migrate elsewhere, as employees not working in lockstep with your purpose may be more of a drain on the organization than a benefit.

When an organization is open to discovering their purpose, magical things can happen. Look at Chicago's Lyric Opera. They knew they needed to become more relevant and were willing to recreate their story from the inside out. Their team threw themselves wholeheartedly into the Discover process and we spent quite some time listening to their stories. Then Adam made a suggestion that electrified the room. Their real Why, he suggested, is "Igniting transformation through art." That captured it, and as you'll see in their case study in Appendix B, the freethinking opera company wasted no time moving forward to the Ignite stage.

Ignite

For Millennials (and other generations, for that matter), an enlightened company offers more than a substantial paycheck and fringe benefits. People want to feel inspired and feel they have a purpose. How does a corporate founder or CEO excite and motivate his Tribe and provide those human benefits? We venture to suggest that the True Purpose Institute has got it right when they say that first is helping each person develop as an individual; second is following a greater purpose; and third is developing a system such as holacracy, which empowers all employees to take a leadership role and make meaningful decisions.[49]

There is no perfect formula for igniting a conscious culture. But there must be mutual trust, which is one of the pillars of mindfulness. And the way you ignite a conscious culture must take advantage of the inherent human need to socialize and be productive. The organization's leader needs to display genuine vulnerability and transparency. He or she needs to open up and level the playing field and be serious about the company's people becoming true partners. A 30-minute town hall once a year doesn't cut it anymore. The traditional top-down management structure must be turned topsy-turvy. The message: there needs to be motivation from within.

ARCA is an example: they're a company that makes hardware and software products designed to help other businesses handle payments more securely and efficiently. To anyone in the creative space, this might not sound too exciting. But you can tell ARCA doesn't fit the mold when you see this statement on their website: "At ARCA we are dedicated to the

---

[49] "How It Works," Holacracy, https://www.holacracy.org/how-it-works/.

BRAND IS A REFLECTION OF CULTURE

science of making doohickeys and whatchamacallits work, so you don't have to."[50] As you might expect from a company with such a tongue-in-cheek sense of humor, ARCA ignited change from within by embracing holacracy.

Express

This is where branding and marketing intersects. It's where the ability to express your story is paramount so you and your Tribe can most effectively engage customers and clients. The best marketers are the best storytellers—those who blend art and science, passion and personality; individuals who grab an audience's attention with a tale that fascinates and resonates, where they share your experience because you vividly recount that experience. They're standing in your shoes and seeing it through your eyes: eyes that don't glaze over because you bombard them with facts and figures, percentages and statistics, charts and graphs. As we've discussed, there is a place for solid information, but you need emotional involvement to really drive your points home. Think Disney Main Street Parade rather than Wall Street stock ticker.

Know your audience. Speak to them in language they understand. Strive for empathy. And transmit your message via every possible medium. Marketing is traditionally focused on how and where to sell products and services. It often doesn't come from a place of purpose or inspiration. Imagine the difference when your marketing is elevated to a place of purpose, which addresses people rather than products. This is how companies in the future will stand out amidst the noise and clutter, how companies will cut through the dizzying volume of information. They will use their words and deeds to express *what they believe* rather than *what they sell*. People who share the same beliefs will notice, be attracted, and make the choice to engage, both internally and externally. Those who believe are much more loyal customers because it is no longer

---

[50] "Our History," ARCA, https://arca.com/company/history.

just a product or service you are selling, but a story that they believe in and want to join.

Impact

What difference does it make? Answer: all the difference in the world. Really. You want to make your mark. You want to contribute. You want to have an impact on the lives and well- being of your fellow Tribe members and fellow citizens. Right? At the end of the day, that's really what it's all about.

When you set out to make a difference you're making quite a statement. It's not enough to develop and manufacture the best widget of its kind; it's not enough to generate stratospheric profits. Your Everest is bettering humankind. Yes, it's quite an aspiration, but why settle for anything less? How big is your Impact going to be? Let us give you an example.

"Make the world a better place." That's some kind of impact. And that's the purpose of Perma-Seal Basement Systems. Serving the Chicagoland and Northwest Indiana areas since.

1979, the company is the industry leader in dry basements, crawl spaces, and healthy homes. Note the ultimate benefit and purpose: healthy homes!

With more than 250 members of their company or Tribe (yes, they already call their workforce a Tribe) it's impossible to monitor or dictate every client engagement, so Perma-Seal creates a culture that rewards people for being mindful and treating a client as they would a family member. They're being invited into someone's home and should act as an honored guest. They believe they have an impact on people's homes, and even the greater world.

It all began when founder Roy Spencer was working for another basement waterproofing company—one that was contributing to the negative reputation earned by much of the industry through unethical business practices and poor customer service. He knew there had to be a better way. Later joined by his wife, Laura Ann Spencer, the company has nurtured a culture of "doing the right thing," which includes offering lifetime warranties and not charging for service calls.

Laura Ann told us, "One of our core values is to 'do what you say you will do.' With our Tribe, we tie actions back to the values. Personal stories resonate with people, which in turn can help guide future actions. We're here to help people have a dry basement and therefore a healthy home."47 And that's how they make their contribution toward making the world a better place.

Summary

Now you have the road map next to you, let's get started inspiring a Tribe of like-minded individuals to work together for the collective good. It's time to explore the different stage more deeply.

THE **SCIENCE** OF **STORY**

CHAPTER 3
Discover

"If you don't go after what you want, you'll never have it. If you don't ask, the answer is always no. If you don't step forward, you're always in the same place."

—*Nora Roberts, Bestselling Author (as J. D. Robb)*

Though the two Israeli teens had only planned to have fun on their class trip, the outdoor backdrop at Auschwitz led to other plans. Here, history flashed before their eyes. Here, their people had nearly been annihilated. Surprisingly, the scarred landscape and tragic past inspired them. Before they left Auschwitz, the two teens, Ofir Fisher and Roni Flamer, promised each other something: to start a movement to bring light into Israel and the world. They felt that if they didn't make life better for those around them and help Israel get stronger and safer, they'd be abdicating their responsibility.

After high school, the young men served time in the army. But instead of remaining in their elite units, dreaming of becoming generals one day, they reunited. Their youthful ambition began crystallizing into something more specific: to define modern Zionism. Lacking an action plan, they decided to travel around Israel. "What do you think it is important to do in Israel and what do you see as the challenges?" they would ask citizens from around the country.

Slowly, an alarming realization grew: Israel's population of approximately eight million was on track to double by 2048. People and wealth were already unhealthily concentrated in the middle of the country; if that imbalance were exacerbated, overcrowding, immovable traffic, and the national housing crisis would spike.

But Ofir and Roni saw a solution hovering within reach. In 1998, about 70 percent of Israel—the Negev and Galilee regions—was under-populated. Inattention and inactivity had kept those areas a desert of sorts. No big organizations were focused there. No national movement aimed for invigoration.

Undeterred, the pair thought if those regions developed into economic centers in their own right, they would draw people out of the overcrowded state center and improve quality of life for the entire Israeli population. This could also inspire a new vision for Israel and better opportunities to the younger generation, or those interested in relocating to Israel from other countries. In other words, Ofir and Roni needed to reinvent modern Israel. They formed a team and named their quest the OR Movement.

They were initially embraced by Ariel Sharon, then Minister of National Infrastructure, who said he was waiting for someone like them to come along. Initially, they started by working on establishing a new community in the Negev Desert, but the Minister had concerns. He didn't want a group of four single guys—the extent of their nonprofit, at that point—to form the basis for a community. So in early 1999, Ofir and Roni were given an ultimatum: they had two months to find 10 to 12 families to join them.

They met with hundreds of families—and quite a bit of skepticism. As they fielded question after question, they started to understand what these families were looking for: most critically information on education. Where are our kids going to study? How much money will it cost? Where? How long is it going to take? They started an information center, won the trust of 14 families, and on April 21, 1999, broke ground and moved into the community. In the Hebrew calendar, it was Israel's Independence Day.

That first community was their internship of sorts. Fast-forward to today, and they have established nine new communities, expanded the 60+ existing communities, relocated more than 40,000 people, and logged 40,000 families (160,000 people) in their database as potential future residents. They're making huge strides toward their goal of guiding

Negev and Galilee to full economic and social sustainability by 2048, with projected populations of 3 million each. Concurrently, they continue to work with the Government to create national plans, engage in massive awareness campaigns, and maintain front-line involvement in dozens of communities and projects.

Their goal, however, should not be confused with their purpose. Ofir and Roni will tell you that their purpose is to build communities where there were none, working to make Israel the best country in the world. Asking themselves *how* to do that led them to the breakthrough about the inherent potential of Negev and Galilee, and it will lead them through more unforeseen difficulties in the future. What will serve them well here and beyond is effectively *aligning* actions (concrete goals) to belief to make it happen.[51]

It takes courage to say and do what you truly believe, which is at the crux of defining the purpose, or Why, of a business. Igniting purpose within an organization and then expressing it externally are the most powerful tools that leaders have. In our own journey of discovery, we've identified three essential characteristics for a corporate Purpose: what we like to call the Bull's Eye of Purpose. Those characteristics are:

- Simple
- Genuine
- Aspirational

Your purpose is the most important story your brand tells. It should be simple enough to be easily understood, genuine enough to connect authentically with your Tribe, and aspirational enough to take action.

Simple

The essence of your Why should be something you can sum up in as few words as possible—no more than five words is a good guide. Why's

---

[51] Ofir Fisher (Executive Vice President and Co-Founder of OR Movement) in discussion with the author, June 2017.

that? For one thing, because it's easier for people to remember. Condensing your core belief into a succinct phrase or two makes you truly crystallize your intent. If you have a long, flowery purpose statement, how many members of your Tribe can recite it? If your answer is "not many," then what's the point?

As Steve Jobs once said, "That's been one of my mantras—focus and simplicity. Simple can be harder than complex. You have to work hard to get your thinking clean to make it simple. But it's worth it in the end because once you get there, you can move mountains."[52]

And you want to move mountains, don't you? Without simplicity, however, you can't have focus. You can't have recollection. And you can't expect it to resonate with and engage the hearts and minds of your Tribe. From philosophy to politics to technology, the power of simplicity is undeniable. Consciously or subconsciously, once we hear a statement that connects in a smooth and unobstructed way, it sticks. We feel it. Take the messages of the presidential candidates in 2016—"Make America Great Again"[53] and "Stronger Together."[54] They were more than simple slogans; they were powerful visions for the future of the country. They were clean and concise messages. For all these reasons, they both resonated.

Go back further in time and consider the United States Constitution, which, in effect, in just 4,543 words (including signatories), mandates what the country stands for. And, of course, it has a memorable preamble declaring the national Why. As the old saying goes, "Keep it simple."

Genuine

Your purpose must be genuine. The leaders of an organization must truly believe their purpose all of the time, not just part of the time. That belief has to be permanent, or at least until the purpose evolves as the business

---

[52] Stephen Nale, "The 100 Greatest Steve Jobs Quotes," *Complex*, October 5, 2012, http://www.complex.com/pop-culture/2012/10/steve-jobs-quotes/.

[53] "About," Trump Pence Make America Great Again, https://www.donaldjtrump.com/about/.

[54] "About Hillary," The Office of Hillary Rodham Clinton, https://www.hillaryclinton.com/about/.

may evolve. Employees of all generations can detect inauthenticity.

You can't fake it. As Jon Wolske, Culture Evangelist at Zappos Insights puts it, "If you want to have long-lasting relationships that are good for business, authenticity is the key. At Zappos.com, we believe that your culture and your brand are two sides of the same coin, and it makes a lot of sense; why would you work so hard to put out one brand image to the world if you aren't able (willing?) to really live it?"[55]

The most tempting time to fake a purpose statement is when you pick up on a trending sentiment—say, saving whales—that could bring momentum to your business if you align yourself with it. We'd be lying if we said there weren't short-term profits to be gained this way. But inauthenticity is always found out, and ultimately will end up unraveling profits. Short-term, fake purpose statements will create a gap between your stated values and your internal culture. Without conviction behind your purpose, you won't be able to live out your values in the organizational design of your company. Employee engagement will decrease and retention will, too. Your short-term profits will fizzle. The decision to be genuine is not only the right thing to do, but is also the profitable thing to do.

Aspirational

In our perpetual quest for meaning, setting goals that are beyond ourselves and that are for a greater purpose are aspirational and inspirational, too. Note: aspiration and inspiration are not of equal importance. The former focuses on an outcome, and desires to take action toward meaningful, long-lasting/long-term change. To be inspired, meanwhile, is to feel emotional stimulation. It's sometimes long-lasting and sometimes not. David Packard, co-founder of Hewlett-Packard, expressed the importance of long-term aspirations perfectly: "Purpose (which should last at least 100 years) should not be confused with specific goals or business strategies

---

[55] Adam Fridman, "5 Undeniable Reasons Brands Are a Reflection of Their Culture," *Inc.*, November 7, 2016.

(which should change many times in 100 years). Whereas you might achieve a goal or complete a strategy, you cannot fulfill a purpose; it's like a guiding star on the horizon, forever pursued but never reached."[56]

You heard that right: your purpose can't be an easily achievable, nor is it a goal. While some may argue that lasting 100 years really pushes the shelf life, the point is this: Purpose should not be a "flavor of the month," nor should it be driven by personality. It should transcend leaders and leadership teams. Similarly, it should be difficult enough that it constantly demands stretch so you'll never get comfortable. Aiming for something unattainable fosters a sense of humility and an appreciation that can lead us to our greatest potential.

Simon Sinek finds game theory helpful in understanding this long-term mindset. Business, he believes, is an *infinite* game. Many companies make the mistake of believing they're in a *finite* game. After all, that's the type of game we're most familiar with: the kind with known players, fixed rules, and an agreed-upon objective to win. At the end of a nine-inning baseball game, Sinek explains, whoever has more runs is declared the winner, and the game is over.[57]

Purpose-driven companies aim to outlast their competition, not to defeat them, but because business is an infinite game. "It has preexisted before every single company on this planet existed, and it will outlast every single company on this planet," Sinek told a crowded room at CreativeMornings in San Diego in October of 2016.[58] "But if you listen to the words of most companies, they don't know the game they're in. They want to 'be #1.' Based on what metrics? Based on what timeframes? Revenues? Market share? Square footage? Number of employees? Based on a quarter? A year?"

---

[56] Jim Collins and Jerry I. Porras, "Building Your Company's Vision," *Harvard Business Review*, September-October 1996, hbr.org/1996/09/building-your-companys-vision.

[57] Simon Sinek, "Understanding the Game We're Playing," filmed October 16, 2016 at CreativeMornings, San Diego, CA, video, https://creativemornings.com/talks/simon-sinek-251/2.

[58] Ibid.

"Think about it from the standpoint of your competition. No one will agree that you won. Any company could say 'I didn't agree to those metrics!' You're not #1. And yet companies are obsessed with 'beating' the competition." He continues, "The great organizations understand that they're playing to stay in the game. And this radically changes the kind of decisions you make and the way you see the world. Infinite players play to be better than themselves. To wake up every single day and say 'How can we make our company a better version of itself today than it was yesterday?'" That is not only what ensures who stays in the game the longest, Sinek says, but that's what ensures you'll find joy. "Because the joy comes not from comparison, but from advancement."[59]

Think about that last statement. If your goal is to win as a company, and you can never really win, can you ever find true happiness? However, if your goal is to continually get better, to strive each day to make your company a better version of the one it was yesterday, then you win a little bit every day. Success is no longer about being at a perceived top, but is about being mentally at the top of who you want to be.

Is your purpose statement angled toward long-term advancement? Lenovo Group, the world's largest computer vendor since 2013, had a catchy tagline: "For Those Who Do," but Quinn O'Brien, the brand lead, admits it didn't reveal much about what the company does or what it stands for.[60] For those who do what? It didn't aspire. It wasn't forward-looking. It wasn't action-oriented. It wasn't until CEO Yang Yuanqing tweeted how they are a company that "never stands still" that Lenovo claimed this phrase as an internal rallying cry that represented the company's relentlessness in all facets of business.[61] They're always moving forward, encouraging their Tribe to seek the unattainable. That's true aspiration, and you need to strive for true aspiration in your Purpose.

---

[59] Ibid.

[60] Quinn O'Brien (Brand Lead at Lenovo Group) in discussion with the author, March 2016.

[61] Adam Fridman, "Do You Know Your Brand Identity? It Starts With Your Why," *Inc.*, February 2, 2016, https://www.inc.com/adam-fridman/do-you-know-your-brand-identity-it-s-start-with-your-why.html.

Questions to Ask

When it comes to constructing your company Why, there are some questions that frequently arise. Oftentimes, people want to know if it makes any difference if your Why sounds too much like that of a competitor.

Our response is that if your Why statement is remarkably similar to that of another organization, you might ask if that's an issue. Maybe not. Perhaps you complement rather than compete with each other. Perhaps there's an opportunity to work together for the greater good. But first do some senior executive soul-searching. Is this your true voice? Your Why needs to be authentic, and as long as it is a genuine reflection of your purpose and not a "Me, too," you should stick with it.

We're also asked: Can you have more than one Why? The bottom line is that you can only have one clear-cut Why at any given time. You can't be chasing down multiple paths to change the world. At Mabbly, we're on the fifth iteration of our Why, and you will probably find that your Why evolves over time with experience and changing circumstances. Remember, your Why is a fit for where you are in your growth, and it is okay to change it as you move forward and your company changes. But whatever your Why is at any given time, you have to be fully dedicated to it.

On a personal level, you may find that your work environment doesn't match your own Why. That can be quite a challenge. What to do? If your own purpose is miles apart from the corporate purpose, it might be time for you to seek a position elsewhere. But remember, most Whys are aspirational, and if there's any possibility for influencing your organization, why not become the agent of change and take control not only of your journey, but your company's journey, too?

If your organization is struggling to agree on its purpose, don't give up. Allocate more time and energy to the project. Be tenacious. There may be members of the Tribe who take a long time to get it, or may never get it, and maybe they just don't belong. Dig deep to discover the source of disagreement. Is it the essence of the message or the words describing the message? You may need to seek outside help resolving the issue as you're simply too close to it. Perhaps you can at least agree that the purpose statement must be simple, genuine, aspirational, and something that has an emotional charge.

Try this: put different Whys on the table and then take a pulse check. Ask your organization to quickly give a natural reaction from one to three; three is the deepest, most positive response and one the least. This way you can tap into your Tribe's emotional subconscious and shape your organization accordingly.

The Discover Test

When you explain your purpose to your Tribe, do they *feel* something? Are they inspired? Enthused? Motivated? If they don't feel anything, you need to keep looking for the right message and the right words. Ask yourself: What's the greatest impact your business could have on the world? Think way beyond holding a volunteer day or writing a big check to charity at the end of the year. Consider your true motives, even for these good deeds. Hint: it can't be just because you think you'll get good media coverage.

If your Tribe is going to contribute blood, sweat, and tears to achieve company goals, they need to identify with the unified greater purpose. More importantly, if your Tribe feels that they contribute to a shared purpose, you have helped them find meaning in their own lives. When the employee, brand, and client align on purpose, everyone can be emotionally compensated by the organization's successes and progressions toward their individual purpose. A shared, inclusive purpose will make employees feel that their physical and emotional effort in serving the organization is rightly rewarded and reciprocated. Building the individual purposes of employees into the organization's purpose will fulfill employees' need to belong and will foster a shared identity and unified direction. It dovetails nicely with Maslow's Hierarchy of Needs, in which love is one of the primary needs on the road to self-actualization.

Does your purpose have to do with your actual product or service? Not necessarily. At the $47 billion multinational delivery service FedEx, purpose aligns with culture in their "Purple Promise" awards and recognition program. FedEx people unite behind the corporate promise to, "Make every FedEx experience outstanding."[62] It's aimed at internal relationships, as well as external customers. Employees who go above and beyond, and demonstrate initiative and problem-solving behavior are saluted through Purple Promise. It's all designed to build customer trust and loyalty and long-term relationships.

Similarly, Arby's brand purpose is, "Inspiring smiles through delicious experiences," a purpose that makes no explicit mention of the food they serve.[63] "We are a 52-year-old brand that began with a purpose," says Chris Fuller, SVP of Brand and Corporate Communications.[64] "Our original founders saw a need to differentiate their product and brand in a crowded marketplace, and today we aim to instill a strong clarity of purpose across our entire brand."[65] This purpose has inspired Arby's charitable work. Since teaming up with Share Our Strength's No Kid Hungry campaign in 2011, Arby's has helped provide more than 460 million meals to children nationwide.[66] The keen sense of purpose at the heart of Arby's organization gives them a reason for existence beyond just serving food to hungry customers.

Getting Started

---

[62] Allen Adamson, "Culture Eats Brand Strategy For Lunch At FedEx," *Forbes*, March 10, 2017, https://www.forbes.com/sites/allenadamson/2017/03/10/culture-eats-brand-strategy-for-lunch-at-fedex/#16c325031863.

[63] "Who We Are and What We Do," Arby's, https://arbys.com/about.

[64] Adam Fridman, "How Your Purpose Answers Why Your Brand Exists," *Inc.*, October 13, 2016, https://www.inc.com/adam-fridman/how-your-purpose-answers-the-reason-for-why-your-brand-exists.html.

[65] Ibid.

[66] Ibid.

You have already heard stories of organizations that have crystallized their corporate purpose in ways that have great impact. How did they arrive at this point? They grappled with questions we put to them (questions that can guide your efforts, as well). They include:

- Who do you consider the stakeholders in your business?

- What do you do?

- How do you do it?

- Why does your organization exist?

We classified responses into three levels of companies:

Level 1. These companies were typically focused on sales: making sales and simply identifying prospects and their target audience/s.

Level 2. These companies (the vast majority) had taken a step forward. They recognized there were two distinct kinds of stakeholders—external and internal. They acknowledged the huge importance of their internal stakeholders—their employees, team members, Tribe (whatever they elected to call them).

Level 3. Only a few companies had progressed to a level in which they look beyond the immediate stakeholder groups and aim to have a bigger impact on the world. All the companies in this level transcend selling and are passionate about the role they play beyond the immediate business goals.

In the next chapter, we delve into the details of the Discover stage, which will benefit organizations at all levels.

CHAPTER 4

The Process to Discover Purpose

"You shouldn't focus on why you can't do something, which is what most people do. You should focus on why perhaps you can, and be one of the exceptions."

—*Steve Case, Co-Founder of AOL*

Military vets often have a tough time transitioning back into society, and that's where Bunker Labs marshals its forces to help. The national not-for-profit organization encourages vets to start their own businesses and connects them to the resources they need—people, financing, and programs.

But Todd Connor, a Navy veteran who served aboard the USS Bunker Hill (CG-52) during Operation Iraqi Freedom, founded this company without having formulated a purpose statement. Once he moved to discover and develop one, he was extremely intentional and deliberate in his efforts.

He told us, "I took the first crack (at the purpose statement) just to give people a sense of the size, scope, and format of how I was thinking about it. Then my team took ownership of it and made tweaks and changes, and then our board did the same thing and ultimately approved it."

He shares that he needed the final statement, to serve as a lens for what we will do, and almost as importantly, what we will 'not' do. If something doesn't feel right or go right, we can go back to our guiding 'Battle Plan' and see how what we were trying to do was not in alignment with our 'why' or our values."

That "Battle Plan," or purpose statement, was to, "Empower veterans as leaders in innovation," says Todd, "We have had lots of imitators to our business model and our organization and the thing that I see, that I am not sure they see, is how we are grounded differently as an organization because of our values and our why. Our grounding in why we do what we do is really differentiated versus our competition (other not for profits, universities, government programs, entrepreneurship programs)."

Bunker Labs has already expanded to 31 employees and $2 million in revenue (donations). Todd says their purpose statement is, "The rallying cry for when things are hard or not working—we at least know *why* we are doing what we are doing."[67]

By picking up this book and allowing yourself the freedom and the opportunity to be curious, you have accepted the responsibility to become a champion of purpose. So, are you ready? Ready to discover your purpose? By now, we trust that you're champing at the bit, eager to get started. And your first question is almost certainly: How long is it going to take? The answer you're probably not going to like: It depends.

Our findings are clear: there is no single path. In fact, the best way to explain the pattern we found is to bring it to a human relationship level. Remember, it is not just about you, whether you are a marketing manager or the CEO, it is about every member of your Tribe. The time it takes to identify your purpose depends on a number of factors:

- **Size of the company.** Understandably, it may be easier to formulate your purpose when you have a small company with fewer employees to involve. You won't be surprised to hear that our conversations with organizations that have more than 40,000 employees scattered across multiple countries, continents, and cultures required more energy and thought. Rebooting is never an easy journey, especially at big companies that have built-in complexities. No matter. All are invited. All can succeed.

- **Existing culture.** How ingrained is your company's current

---

[67] Todd Connor (Navy veteran and Founder of Bunker Labs) in discussion with the author October, 2016.

culture? Are you locked into a mindset because "It's always been this way" and has served you well in the past? Or have you been able to pivot in the past and embrace new concepts? Agile and innovative organizations clearly have an easier time communicating their purpose to their Tribe, and therefore more expediently work through the Express stage and return to it, as needed, as the business evolves.

- **Industry.** The time required is actually not influenced by industry. It just doesn't make a significant difference. There isn't one template for retailers and another for IT folks. When it comes to purpose, people come first, regardless of industry. We find that the pursuit to discover purpose is unique to each organization and its people, not to the industry.

- **Age of the team.** Millennials (Gen Y) fearlessly demand meaning in every aspect of their lives, including their chosen careers. It's in their DNA. They expect purpose to be a core pursuit of companies where they work and brands they support. In general, the younger your Tribe, the more responsive they will be to the pursuit of purpose.

- **Leadership mindset.** Who is going to champion the discovery of purpose? Who is going to embrace wholeheartedly this new way of running a company? Without nimble and conscious leaders creating a fertile ground, the ability to nurture the purpose journey becomes a lot harder.

- **Reason to begin the journey.** Why? Why have you started on this journey? Perhaps there's a sense of urgency because you have been hit with some immediate challenges, which are perceived to stem from lack of purpose. Pressure to change can come from a disconnect with customers, inability to excite prospective team members, or leadership fatigue. It's important to note that to accomplish the vision we set forth in this book, companies must reset and decide to communicate to their Tribe what they believe versus what they do. If a company moves to solve a crisis by creating a short-term tactical plan and a feel-good tagline, it is not a holistic purpose transformation. It does nothing more than bandage the problem.

Now, some good news. Most companies who truly embark on the purpose transformation by allocating necessary mindshare and empowering the process do find what they seek. It may not be perfect the first time around, but that's OK. In fact, iteration may be the new perfect.

Inspired Purpose Champions

How do we start? Our research shows that those who simply have the courage and curiosity to ask this question will succeed, but someone needs to be the initiator.

Take Compass Group for example, a global leader in contract foodservice and hospitality that serves millions of people. Its Morrison Community Living division works with 200 senior living communities. Vice President Travis Young, who oversees this division, told us he decided to make it his mission to challenge the status quo of an industry known for its high turnover, struggling safety scores, and disengagement.

He took on the challenge of trying to get thousands of hourly wage workers across the nation to feel a sense of purpose, in furtherance of the belief that everyone deserves to be celebrated, whether it be a dishwasher or a senior executive. He made sure that at the Morrison Community, every new hire starts on a Tuesday and their first experience is a surprise welcome party followed by the instruction to take the rest of the day off! On their first day, they're also presented with a small, but mighty, plastic card that will define the rest of their days at the company.

The card is a reminder of Morrison's "Did You?" culture. Every employee, Travis included, carries it at all times. It is a part of the company uniform and serves as a reminder that everyone in the organization has the power to provide value every day. It asks questions such as, "Did you train someone today?" and "Did you keep your team safe today?"

Whether it's adding value to people, operational excellence, or financial responsibility, Morrison Community Living employees are expected to hold themselves to a higher standard and know that they, and their jobs, are about more than just a paycheck. Unlike some of the other divisions that have yet to adopt the "Did You?" culture, they have seen a change for the better:

- A 5–9 percent reduction in turnover

- Increased engagement scores

- Growth of 15–17 percent for three straight years

- International Food Safety Score moved from 5.22 to 1.89 (The lower the score, the better: industry standard is 3.0)[68]

For Morrison Community Living, it started with one purpose champion who embraced change and reached as far as he could. The result was serious impact. Even one small change can be the butterfly effect that impacts individuals and your organization, and continues to have an impact well beyond the company's walls.

Step one is putting together a team to lead the efforts. We call them "Inspired Purpose Champions" (IPC). They are dedicated individuals who champion the Discover process through the system. It's vital that they are given a wide degree of organizational empowerment and authority to facilitate a successful outcome in the shortest time possible. They facilitate the process by nurturing feedback, radiating it throughout the company, and establishing organization-wide buy-in. This is why your IPC should become the beating heart of the organization while a Purpose Thesis is

---

[68] Travis Young (Vice President of Compass Group Morrison Community Living division) in discussion with the author, June 2017.

developed.

Once that Thesis is validated (possibly after going through multiple iterations), you will have found your Purpose. Considering the critical success factors (discussed below) upfront should facilitate your success.

1. Size of IPC Group. Depending on the size of your organization, the IPC group should consist of three to nine people. With larger organizations, the sheer magnitude of stakeholders requires enormous bandwidth for continued communication. We recommend an odd number to avoid stalemates.

2. Cross-Functional. Ideally, IPC will represent different areas of the business. Marketing, Finance/Accounting, HR, and Operations should be included to offer their various perspectives.

3. Empowerment. Either through inclusion of a senior leader (ideally the founder or CEO), or through mandate, it must be clear IPCs are on a mission critical initiative within the organization.

4. Deeply Engaged. It is beneficial to include experienced and engaged team members to ensure they have a positive outlook toward the work of the IPC group.

5. Unleash Creativity. This team is tasked to find the organization's true purpose. It's essential to recognize that it is not a structured or linear process. To unlock creativity, the team should explore holding meetings at various locations—from casual jams at coffee shops to retreats at offsite locations. The best ideas are stimulated when there's a paradigm shift in all aspects, from physical venue to the content of the exchange. The goal is to unhinge from the status quo and the everyday flow.

6. Stakeholder Mapping. Before IPC really gets underway, you need to go through a stakeholder mapping exercise to make sure there's alignment between all the stakeholder groups. Depending on the size of the organization, you may subdivide into seniority, experience, areas of responsibility, or other characteristics. This could include owners, investors, and the Board. Ideally, some form of stakeholder mapping should have been completed before this point, but the exercise by IPCs has value because it does foster alignment and ownership.

Purpose Jams

What are "Purpose Jams?" They are sessions for internal stakeholders (guided by IPCs that are designed to inspire the creation of a Purpose Thesis.

Purpose discussions require an elevated, almost transcendent, state of mind. Remember when our parents said, "You can be anything you want to be when you grow up?" We didn't have context at the time to understand the power and unlimited possibilities of this statement. We do now. How epic is this feeling? Your organization is about to find the real reason for its existence, and, through a domino effect, the energy will propagate through every cell of the organism and ecosystem.

Ideally, most of the members of the organization would go through the process and the results would be documented and cataloged for the Purpose Thesis. We've found that crowd-sourced purposes have the highest chance of enduring and the least amount of resistance from the participants.

Conducting a Purpose Jam

In the first instance, the IPC team should conduct its own Purpose Jam—our inspiration-to-action workshops. IPC members should exhibit boldness and take a leap of faith by exploring different options as they work their way toward establishing their own Purpose Thesis. Start the meeting with a blank canvas and don't go the easy route of starting with an existing premise. We recommend beginning a journal to document ideas and reasons for pivots as you embark on the most important journey of your brand. Once they understand the process, individual IPC members should orchestrate Purpose Jams throughout the organization. Here's our suggested overview to put together your own Purpose Jam:

1. Environment. Pick a space that encourages creativity. It must have white boards or other areas where thoughts and ideas can be written down to give participants a clear visual of the progress.

2. Time. Allocate at least one hour of focused and uninterrupted attention. When taking part in this session, it doesn't serve anyone's best interests to operate with a speed chess mindset. What's optimal is a relaxed, soul-searching state. You may wish to start with a simple breathing exercise or a few minutes of meditation to set the right mood. While you certainly should have a focus, forget about making a rigid schedule. Remarkable ideas bubble up when you dispense with a step-by-step agenda.

3. Craziness Welcomed. Make it clear at the onset that this is a no-holds-barred, free-thinking, free-wheeling session. Participants should not feel constrained in any way. The process may be guided, but the outcome is unknown. In fact, it is perfectly OK if this session ends with more questions than answers. This step is the beginning.

4. No Seniority. Everyone has an equal say. It is critical to level the playing field for this session. Any seniority-dominated pressures will hinder the genuine contribution from all participants and will negatively impact the outcome. Everyone's voice needs to be given equal weight. You never know where a great idea will come from.

5. Inspire. How can you motivate participants to wholeheartedly wrap their arms around the search for the organizational purpose? We recommend that you pick some of the case studies in Appendix B (the segments we call "They Live It") and use them to open the session. Showing and telling real world examples like these will break many paradigms and unlock a universe of possibilities.

Alternatively, use the questions in this starter script (below) to kick things off. The goal is to help people in the room find the overlap between what they're passionate about and what the company's good at doing.

- Why did you join this company?
- What gets you motivated in the morning?
- When are you most likely to enter your flow state?
- If you could change the world, what would you change?
- What would your obituary say about you?
- When do you feel most proud of this organization?
- Who embodies the essence of our culture? What are their characteristics?

It is very important to encourage open flow and for the rest of the group either to stay silent or assist in asking follow-up questions. Depth here is very beneficial.

6. Insight. Once everyone's contribution has been gathered, pause and evaluate the responses. Most of the initial responses will be inward-facing rather than an aspiration to impact the world at large. Do not bias the results by acknowledging with your IPC group that you expected this perspective. In other words, acting without an established greater purpose, your IPCs will typically respond (inwardly) within one of the following categories:

- Team: appreciation for the team's work, collaboration, ideation, family-oriented environment.
- Customer-centric: enjoyment in helping the customer, building relationships, solving challenges, making an impact.
- Personal growth: being challenged, making progress, personal development from technical to interpersonal.

Commenting on (at the right time) the contrast between an inward perspective and the desired greater purpose will help everyone in the room reflect on the difference between having greater purpose and not having it. Without a reason for being that expands beyond your organization's walls, you will likely focus your attention on your everyday experiences at work. There is nothing wrong with that. However, we don't think that settling for this inward focus reaches the ultimate and transcendent state that unifies and ignites the type of action that can change the world.

7. Purpose Thesis. Once you have worked your way through the above steps, the IPC group is now ready to go after the real question, "Why does our organization exist?" It is important to explain what the Bull's Eye of Purpose looks like, as explained in the Discover chapter. If time allows, conduct a two-minute tutorial around the concepts of "Simple. Genuine. Aspirational" shared earlier. Now, let's unleash the brainstorm. Emphasize that no idea is too big and there are absolutely no limits.

The output of the Purpose Jam will include individual Whys and a brainstorm toward the organization's Purpose Thesis. The results of each session should be consolidated by the IPC into a master document such as a mind map that is all-inclusive. The fact that members of the Tribe have not only been included, but also heard, begins to build ownership of the greater reason for being. Every team member will leave the session feeling uplifted and in deep reflection of their own meaning, as well as the company's purpose.

Once the top candidates for the Purpose Thesis are identified, it is time to share them and see how they resonate with more team members. In our experience, presenting an Aspirational, Simple, and Genuine purpose without a story that's inspiring is an incomplete presentation. Your audience will not have the context or the anchors to fully appreciate this bigger, broader framing.

For instance, Griffith Foods, a product development partner specializing in food ingredients, caught us off-guard with the story behind their purpose in what turned out to be one of our most intense, emotional, and awe-inspiring interviews. When we asked about their purpose, without any hesitation—unlike many interviews we've carried out with other companies—owner and chairman Brian Griffith responded, "We blend care and creativity to nourish the world."

We suggested that rather than talking about what they did—"Blending care and creativity"—they consider a more aspirational alternative: "We believe in nourishing the world." After a moment of reflection, TC Chatterjee, CEO, countered, "That's a belief system. It's not actionable, and it is not enough to just believe in it."[69] The Griffith leadership team prefers having action verbs in their purpose as a commitment to their employees, their partners, the community, and the world. As we dug deeper, curious where such conviction came from, we realized that their gift to the world had been passed down through generations. As the fourth-generation Griffith to run the business, it was no surprise the meeting became emotional when Brian spoke of lessons instilled in him by his father Dean Griffith, who passed away in 2016.

"My parents taught me the company is a vehicle for the greater good," Brian told us. So, he took his father's idea and aspiration and, as he assumed more global leadership in the company, pursued the transformation process, determined to turn the concept into reality. It was important to him that there was more than hope—that there was a concrete structure to implement the corporate purpose. He has continued his focus on embedding this structure at every level of the organization.[70]

In his 2006 memoir, his father Dean wrote, "Just as transformation occurs in nature, it also occurs in business. Knowledge from the past is recycled and transformed by the demands of new situations ."[71] Brian had

---

[69] TC Chatterjee (Chief Executive Officer at Griffith Foods) in discussion with the author, August 2017.
[70] Brian Griffith (Chairman of the Board at Griffith Foods) in discussion with the author, August 2017.
[71] "Remembering Dean Griffith," Griffith Foods, http://www.griffithfoods.com/whoweare/Pages/Dean.aspx.

taken his knowledge of his father's vision and acted on it, and committed to a purpose statement of continuing action.

As we've discussed, delivering your story is the means of having the most impact. It's the way to connect, resonate, and inspire; it's the way to convey the message that you believe in something greater than a product or a solution. How do you accomplish that?

Internal Media Hubs

Internal communication tools like emails, private intranets, and even onboarding training can all communicate purpose, but one challenge with all of them is that they don't sustain ongoing engagement. All too often, buy-in never extends beyond the executive suite either, because the stated purpose doesn't really fit with the Tribe's lived experience of the company (i.e., what you say and what you do don't line up), or because the purpose is not communicated effectively.

Here's a better solution for communicating purpose to your Tribe: an internal media hub. A hub is more than a blog or a webpage. It's a place for organizations to share their stories and define what makes them tick. An internal media hub is a place to engage with your Tribe and allow them to engage with each other; it's a place where purpose is communicated on an ongoing basis. There will be a lot more on internal media hubs in the next chapter.

Perhaps you are saying to yourself that an internal media hub sounds similar to an intranet site. You're right—the concepts are similar. Both involve putting content online for employees to browse. The difference is in how it's done. Whereas a company intranet provides an opportunity for the organization to push information *at* employees, a hub exists as a place to develop community. Employees can contribute to a hub in ways they cannot contribute with a static intranet site. An internal media hub is also more robust and engaging. It can be accessed from any device, it invites participation, and it can provide a multimedia platform on which to share company videos, podcasts, notes, and other content.

A few other key differences between an internal media hub and your old static intranet:

- **Content is oriented around purpose.** Orienting your content around purpose doesn't mean simply having a bunch of articles that ramble on about purpose. It means the content supports *why* you do what you do, not just the how or the what. In practice, this means the content ties in to purpose in some meaningful way.

- **The site and content are branded.** Your internal media hub is more than a private website for sharing memos and policies with employees. It should reflect the idea that you are curating content for, by, and about your Tribe in a way that fits clearly with the goals you want to achieve. Think of it as an internal online magazine that supports and promotes your purpose.

- **Crowd-sourced stories from around your company.** Your hub should deliver insights from members of the Tribe at all levels of the organization, not just your leadership team. Crowd-sourced or community-sourced content has multiple advantages: it's less expensive to produce, it delivers numerous and varied points of view from around your company, and it can highlight and help solve problems. Another added benefit? Employees are naturally more engaged with stories about themselves and their peers, especially when they themselves have an opportunity to contribute.

- **An internal media hub is multimedia and multiplatform.** Because more than half of website visits now come from mobile devices, your internal media hub should be available across multiple platforms to allow your Tribe to visit at the times and locations that are most convenient for them. And, to maximize engagement, the hub shouldn't consist solely of text content. It should be able to handle images, video, audio, and more.

Why Do You Need an Internal Media Hub?

A hub is essentially a gathering place or online water cooler where Tribe members can connect at a time that's convenient for them. Or if you prefer this analogy: think of members of a Tribe sitting around a campfire and sharing stories. Internal media hubs respond to key organizational needs by helping to develop and promote the connections that often go missing, especially as growing numbers of employees work remotely in field offices or from home. A few of the benefits of internal media hubs include:

- Giving employees a voice: especially important in companies where employees are widely distributed.
- Creating community: internal media hubs facilitate the development of relationships among employees, managers, and executives, regardless of their location or place on the corporate totem pole.
- Engage over time: email has a short shelf life; intranet sites tend to be text heavy, top down, and boring. Hubs are available over time, across multiple platforms, and provide a more consistent home for your message.

Whether it's learning about events going on around the company, recognizing and rewarding employees for their achievements, or facilitating communication among executives, managers and employees, hubs help organizations achieve greater engagement.

At Levenfeld Pearlstein, LLC, a Chicago-based legal firm, the company's InfoHub is an essential tool, says Andrea Maciejewski, Director of Client Engagement. She told us, "Internal communications are frequently overlooked, and that's a critical mistake, because well-informed internal audiences are more productive and can be an organization's best brand ambassadors. Our internal hub allows us to engage employees by promoting their activities and wins, and delivers an efficient means of information sharing and trust-building. When your Tribe trusts management and each other, they are far more productive. Arming them with information allows them to serve better, sell better, and be most engaged."[72]

Although cost can be a barrier, there are many affordable platforms, including WordPress, which can be adopted. By allowing employees to contribute content, the cost of creation is minimized while employee engagement is increased. It's a win-win.

Once an organization finds and communicates its purpose internally, the following become more likely:

1. Spark. Tribe members who resonate with the organization's purpose and trust its legitimacy will realize a personal transformation. We like to call it, "Getting wind under your wings." Transformation will be from within and Tribe members will find themselves living-to-work instead of working-to-live. In fact, "work" as a concept takes an entirely different meaning when we believe in what we do. This state is more than mental. As we mentioned earlier, our body chemistry undergoes physical changes. For instance, when someone places their trust in us or shows us an act of kindness, the feel-good chemical oxytocin is released. Hear an inspiring, motivating story and dopamine, which makes us feel more hopeful and optimistic, is produced.

2. Evolution. Where is the connection between individual purpose and organizational purpose? How does an individual decide if they belong in the organization? We believe there should be a strong connection between a person's and organization's reason for being. This is what forms unity in a team. While many members of your team will enthusiastically embrace a newly stated purpose, others, inevitably, will react negatively. We are all different, and what creates immense

---

[72] Andrea Maciejewski (Director of Client Engagement at Levenfeld Pearlstein, LLC) in discussion with the author, March 2016.

passion in one person may well scare someone else. Individuals in the latter group will feel disconnected and displaced. In fact, with every escalation in intensity toward the newly found North Star, this disconnected group will feel more and more lost, and some will voluntarily leave the organization. The departure of some personnel is perfectly natural and should be anticipated and welcomed. It's a sign that they weren't a good fit for this team. You should celebrate the end of their season and then search for others who are going to be in sync with your purpose.

The Takeaway

Once you've done the work of homing in on your purpose, one of the most important steps your company will need to take is finding ways to communicate that purpose to your Tribe across time and distance. Internal media hubs provide a means of doing this that is both cost effective and engaging. You may be surprised how ready your Tribe is to participate.

Which leads us to the next stage of Ignite—the importance of firing up the members of your Tribe to fully commit to venture on this voyage with you.

CHAPTER 5
Ignite

"The value of an idea lies in the using of it."

—*Thomas Edison, Inventor*

In pursuing our own journey, we were surprised to discover how many companies articulated a clearly stated purpose and set of company values, but had an obvious disconnect when it came to the actual implementation of the values. Companies may have had purpose statements written in pretty words, but there was no habitual action. There were no underlying habits that members of their Tribe automatically performed day in and day out. They didn't walk the talk.

Ignition begins at home. Once you have found your company's purpose, the next step before broadcasting it to the world is to make sure all the members of your Tribe are on board. This is where culture comes in: employees are 1.4 times more engaged at purpose-driven companies,[73] and companies with a culture of engagement outperform their peers by 147 percent.[74]

Meanwhile, according to Gallup polls, more than 85 percent of workers worldwide—and more than 65 percent of American workers—say they feel disengaged at work.[75] Look around you. What does this mean? Nearly four out of five of your colleagues is so turned off that their poor attitude

---

[73] "Winning with Purpose," EY Entrepreneurial Winning Women Conference, accessed November 28, 2017. http://www.ey.com/Publication/vwLUAssets/EY-purpose-led-organizations/$FILE/EY-purpose-led-organizations.pdf.

[74] "The Engaged Workplace," Gallup, accessed November 28, 2017. http://www.gallup.com/services/190118/engagedworkplace.aspx?gclid=CIn487iJxM4CFdBZhgodhi4G2w.

[75] Steve Crabtree, "Worldwide, 13 percent of Employees Are Engaged at Work," *Gallup News*, October 8, 2013, http://news.gallup.com/poll/165269/worldwide-employees-engaged-work.aspx.

is probably spreading like a virus. They are, in effect, working against the company's objectives. This can have a disastrous impact on productivity, morale, and employee retention. Never mind the fact that you won't get new employees from positive word-of-mouth referrals. All of this leaves companies in a persistent state of catch-up.

Engaged employees, however, can make a 180-degree difference. A chief scientist at Gallup, Jim Harter, Ph.D., sums it up nicely. He writes: "Engaged employees are more attentive and vigilant. They look out for the needs of their coworkers and the overall enterprise, because they personally 'own' the result of their work and that of the organization." They "help people see the connection between their everyday work and the larger purpose or mission of the organization."[76] Sounds like the janitor who felt he was helping to put a man on the moon.

Here, a word of warning. Just as happiness is elusive to those who want it too desperately, employee engagement can't be addressed head-on. Perhaps we can look at employee engagement as we look at laughter: you don't pursue it, but it is the outcome of humor. Similarly, engagement is a pursuit of something deeper; for us, it's purpose. You have to get to the root of the problem. And to clarify, we have seen many organizations approach purpose through redesign of their office. We absolutely agree, space is an important consideration and in the words of Cheryl Durst, the Executive Vice President and CEO of the International Interior Design Association (IIDA), "The focus is on design and space being a reflection of culture."[77] However, Cheryl believes, "Designers are amazing at diagnosing culture and finding the right space for you. However they can not fix a culture issue." We concluded that, "Great culture happens when organizations ask their people the right questions, and connect with them in a human way—through relationship, purpose, and opportunity. It happens when

---

[76] John Baldoni, "Employee Engagement Does More than Boost Productivity," *Harvard Business Review*, July 4, 2013, https://hbr.org/2013/07/employee-engagement-does-more.

[77] Cheryl Durst (Executive Vice President and CEO of the International Interior Design Association) in discussion with the author, July 2016.

organizations motivate and empower, rather than mandate behavior."[78]

By now, you might be confused and rightly so. First we were talking about purpose and now we're talking about culture. Aren't they two separate things? Isn't one about long-term business strategy and one about organizational design? Take the Kellogg (food) Company's purpose: "Nourishing families so they can flourish and thrive."[79] That's an inspirational direction, but does it provide any rules for the company's organizational design?

It's true that purpose and values are different beasts. In a *Harvard Business Review* article titled, "Your Company's Purpose Is Not Its Vision, Mission, or Values," Graham Kenny, President of Reinvent Australia, distinguished between purpose, which can be defined as a, "Way to express the organization's impact on the lives of customers, clients, students, patients—whomever you're trying to serve" and values, which, "Describe the desired culture."[80] Whole Foods' values, for instance, include self-directed teams, open and timely information, sustainable agriculture, and inviting store environments. Meanwhile, Whole Foods' stated purpose is, "To co-create a world where each of us, our communities and our planet can flourish. All the while, celebrating the sheer love and joy of food."[81]

As Kenny states, there are, "Already a host of labels out there that describe organizational direction."[82] Do you really need a purpose *and* a set of values? The answer will not surprise you: yes. Purpose and values are intimately related. An organization's purpose is a people-first commitment to the outside world; an organization's values are a people-

---

[78] Adam Fridman, "Transforming Life at Work: Inspiring Culture and Influencing Engagement Within the Workplace," *Inc.*, October 4, 2017, https://www.inc.com/adam-fridman/transforming-life-at-work-inspiring-culture-influencing-engagement-within-workplace.html.

[79] "Our Vision & Purpose," Kellogg's, http://www.kelloggcompany.com/en_US/our-vision-purpose.html.

[80] Graham Kenny, "Your Company's Purpose Is Not Its Vision, Mission, or Values," *Harvard Business Review*, September 3, 2014, https://hbr.org/2014/09/your-companys-purpose-is-not-its-vision-mission-or-values.

[81] "Our Core Values," Whole Foods Market, http://www.wholefoodsmarket.com/mission-values/core-values.

[82] Ibid.

first commitment to both the outside world and the inside world. You couldn't accomplish the latter without the former. Whole Foods believes that in order to help the world flourish (their purpose), they must promote open and timely information (one of their values).[83] Once you know your purpose, you need to figure out how to get there—and that's where values come in.

We're going to say something you might find shocking, given our self-declared obsession with purpose: a purpose statement by itself doesn't mean much. Well, it means both a lot and a little. It commits to making a positive impact on the world, but it doesn't necessarily stop you from making a negative impact on the world. Take Uber's stated purpose to, "Make transportation as reliable as running water, everywhere, for everyone."[84] The purpose neither prohibits nor allows the mistreatment of female employees—which is exactly what Uber was doing, as former Software Engineer Susan Fowler revealed in an explosive blog post titled "Reflecting On One Very, Very Strange Year At Uber." HR representatives refused to punish high-performing men who sexually harassed women, and HR even aided in the cover-up of shockingly inappropriate behavior by telling multiple women who complained about one manager that it was, "His first offense."[85]

Uber customers felt betrayed when Fowler's revelations went live. Implicit in any purpose that commits to serving others over making a profit is the commitment to value all humans, both inside and outside of the organization. But until values are spelled out and woven into policies, the purpose statement remains a narrow directive.

For purpose-driven companies to be seen as authentic, they must enact human-centric values. For instance, if it came to light that Kellogg,

---

[83] "We Support Team Member Happiness and Excellence," Whole Foods, http://www. wholefoodsmarket.com/mission-values/core-values/we-support-team-member-excellence-and-happiness.

[84] "Our trip history," Uber, https://www.uber.com/our-story/.

[85] Susan Fowler, "Reflecting On One Very, Very Strange Year At Uber," *Susan Fowler*, February 19, 2017, https://www.susanjfowler.com/blog/2017/2/19/reflecting-on-one-very-strange-year-at-uber.

whose purpose is, "Nourishing families so they can flourish and thrive," only provided junk food to their single employees, customers would immediately call out their hypocrisy. "Authenticity of corporate purpose happens when there is alignment between a firm's perceived and stated corporate purpose and the actual strategic decisions and actions a firm takes," found the PR firm Burson-Marsteller in a 2015 study.[86]

This is why Etsy, a company devoted to supporting local communities, created an employee food program called "Eatsy." Twice a week, everyone enjoys food made by local vendors (think five-spice pork belly sandwiches and vegan sushi with miso soup).[87] "It would be hypocritical for Etsy to say they believe in supporting local makers and local communities while creating an environment in which employees never have reason to leave their office or frequent local restaurants," said Will Robb, Etsy's Global Food Program Manager.[88]

Employees who engage in strategic thinking about how to apply your purpose more broadly are worth their weight in gold. A survey led by the social enterprise firm Imperative in conjunction with New York University found that while only 28 percent of the workforce was purpose-oriented, these workers were 50 percent more likely to be in leadership positions, 47 percent more likely to be promoters of their employers and have 64 percent higher levels of job fulfillment.[89]

One of the study's principals was Andrew Hurst. He wrote that "The goal is to have leaders across sectors understand the science of purpose in

---

[86] "'Keeping It Real'- Burson-Marsteller and IMD Business School Identify Drivers of Corporate Authenticity," *Burson-Marsteller*, April 14, 2015, http://www.burson-marsteller.com/news/press-release/keeping-it-real-burson-marsteller-and-imd-business-school-identify-drivers-of-corporate-authenticity/.

[87] Aleksa Brown, "Company Culture: Gathering Around the Table at Etsy," *Etsy Journal*, November 28, 2012, https://blog.etsy.com/en/gathering-around-the-table-at-eatsy/.

[88] Mollie West and McCoubrey Judson, "Want to Strengthen Workplace Culture? Design a Ritual," *HuffPost*, December 6, 2017, https://www.huffingtonpost.com/great-work-cultures/want-to-strengthen-workpl_b_11730914.html.

[89] "2015 Workforce Purpose Index," *Imperative*, 2015, accessed November 28, 2017, https://cdn.imperative.com/media/public/Purpose_Index_2015.

the workforce and begin to use it to help boost the performance and well-being of their teams."[90] In other words, since purpose statements ask us to do difficult work, leaders need to strategize about how to protect their employees' well-being. Then they must implement those values through organizational design and corporate strategy. When leaders do a good job, they have engaged employees who feel psychologically safe in their jobs and fulfilled by their work.

Here's the kicker, according to Dr. Andrew Wittman, author of *Ground Zero Leadership*, companies often misunderstand what drives employee engagement, and some efforts to improve it are actively making it worse.

It's no secret that workplaces are dealing with what Gallup calls a 'worldwide employee engagement crisis,' with four of every six employees on the payroll just collecting a check or worse, actively sabotaging the organization. To combat this, the conventional wisdom was to create a company culture around employee satisfaction by offering perks and benefits like child care, gym memberships, robust retirement plans, health insurance and holiday bonuses. It turns out, those things didn't produce engaged employees. Worse, in some ways, they encouraged the disengaged to stay on the payroll by adding what some workplace experts refer to as 'golden handcuffs.'[91]

Because the causes of employee engagement are so poorly understood, too many companies have climbed on the bandwagon of being a purpose-driven company without truly living it and without getting the members of their workforce on board with it. They know that many consumers demand a company have a cause, especially the Millennial generation. So, they pay lip service. They create statements that avow their purpose, but, in fact, are little more than clichés dreamed up in an afternoon of brainstorming. They create statements that are nothing more than empty slogans.

---

[90] Devin Thorpe, "New Report: 'Purpose-Oriented' Employees 'Outperform,'" *Forbes*, December 22, 2015, https://www.forbes.com/sites/devinthorpe/2015/12/22/4988/#23c092813211.

[91] Andrew D. Wittman, "Stop Trying To Make Your Employees Happier," *Entrepreneur*, November 14, 2017, https://www.entrepreneur.com/article/302315.

We'll go into more detail about how to integrate your purpose with your organizational design later in this chapter. We'll argue that while there's leeway to choose specific values, certain human-first policies must be in place in a workplace that claims to care about its employees. But first, a word on your environment.

Culture

What is culture? Essentially, a society's culture is created through the sharing of ideas and passing the best of the best down to younger generations. It's not a uniquely human trait. Consider the Japanese macaque (muk-kak) monkeys. In the early 1950s, scientists studying them on the island of Koshima watched one young female do something new. Before eating sweet potatoes, she dipped them into the river to wash off the sand. You might think that's nothing special, but none of her elders had thought to do it before.[92]

It wasn't long before members of her family and then others began "aping" her. The behavior spread throughout the entire colony of macaques. Later, the female monkey hit on the novel idea of washing the potatoes in the ocean, giving them a saltier, more flavorful taste. That breakthrough caught on as well. Today, washing the potatoes is an activity routinely undertaken by all the macaques. It became part of their culture—a method of passing on habits and customs not so different from the way human culture develops. When humans share inspired ideas with one another, there are truly no limits to what we can accomplish (including a thousand diverse ways to cook potatoes!).[93]

In the business world, culture is a living, breathing organism that emerges from the social and psychological environment within your company.

---

[92] Alfred K., "Monkeys Washing Potatoes," *Alfred*, April 2013, http://alfre.dk/monkeys-washing-potatoes/.
93 Ibid.

THE SCIENCE OF STORY

Culture includes the organization's purpose, beliefs, assumptions, values, and habits and is the key contributor to your organization's effectiveness and competitiveness. Lou Gerstner, former Chairman and CEO of IBM, who is largely credited with turning around the $80 billion Goliath, concluded, "I came to see, in my time at IBM, that culture isn't just one aspect of the game, it is the game."[94]

In the financial services realm, a perceived decline in culture can negatively impact the biggest of names. When Greg Smith, an Executive Director at Goldman Sachs, resigned in 2012, he took to the pages of *The New York Times* and wrote an op-ed piece slamming the Wall Street firm. In his controversial piece, he wrote, "Culture was always a vital part of Goldman Sachs's success. It revolved around teamwork, integrity, a spirit of humility, and always doing right by our clients. The culture was the secret sauce that made this place great and allowed us to earn our clients' trust for 143 years."[95]

Announcing his departure, Smith went on to add, "I am sad to say that I look around today and see virtually no trace of culture that made me love working for this firm for many years. I no longer have the pride, or the belief." He urged the board of directors, "Weed out the morally bankrupt people, no matter how much money they make for the firm. And get the culture right again, so people want to work here for the right reasons. People who care only about making money will not sustain this firm—or the trust of its clients—for very much longer."[96]

In his subsequent book, Smith seems to blame the alleged demise of Goldman Sachs's culture on its transformation from a partnership to a publicly traded company. But you don't have to go public to degenerate from being a culturally thriving company to a culturally deprived company.

---

[94] Dennis Elenburg, Book Review: "Who Says Elephants Can't Dance?" IBM, May 15, 2003, https://www.ibm.com/developerworks/rational/library/2071.html.
[95] Greg Smith, "Why I Am Leaving Goldman Sachs," *The New York Times*, March 14, 2012, http://www.nytimes.com/2012/03/14/opinion/why-i-am-leaving-goldman-sachs.html.
[96] Ibid.

You don't want to lose your 'secret sauce.' That's because when your culture is strong, productive, and purposeful, your organization will enjoy:

- Alignment among Tribe members toward achieving purpose and goals.[97]
- High employee engagement and identification with the Tribe.[98]
- Added attractiveness to quality applicants and improved retention of key talent.[99]
- Increased cohesiveness among the company's departments.[100]
- Higher employee well-being, self-efficacy, and potential for personal growth.[101]
- More consistency, coordination, and control within the company.[102]
- Better employee habits and improved efficiency.[103]
- Stronger overall profitability, growth, and innovation.[104]

Let's now start to think about how we can get your Tribe aligned to the organization's purpose. This is where values guide us toward our goal.

Values Guide

Values, when properly framed—and lived—by an organization, represent the beliefs that definitively define its culture. Values can run the gamut of communication, innovation, teamwork, and loyalty.

But what difference do they make? How important are the values that

[97] Ian N. Lings and Dr R. F. Brooks, "Implementing and Measuring the Effectiveness of Internal Marketing," *Journal of Marketing Management* 14, no. 4/5 (1998): 325-351.

[98] Khanyapuss Punjaisri and Alan Wilson, "The role of internal branding in the delivery of employee brand promise," *Journal of Brand Management* 15, no. 1 (2007): 57-70.

[99] Kristie A. Abston PhD and Virginia W. Kupritz PhD, "Employees as customers: Exploring service climate, employee patronage, and turnover," *Performance Improvement Quarterly* 23, no. 4 (2011): 7-26.

[100] George G. Gordon and Nancy DiTomaso, "Predicting Corporate Performance From Organizational Culture," *Journal of Management Studies* 29, no. 6 (1992): 783-798.

[101] Malcolm Patterson, Peter Warr, and Michael West, "Organizational Climate and Company Productivity: The Role of Employee Affect and Employee Level," *Journal of Occupational and Organizational Psychology* 77, no. 2 (2004): 193-216.

[102] Gordon, George G. and Nancy DiTomaso, "Predicting Performance," 783-798.

[103] Patterson, Malcolm, Peter Warr, and Michael West, "Organizational Climate," 193-216

[104] Roland Calori and Philippe Sarnin, "Corporate Culture and Economic Performance: A French Study," Organization Studies 12, no. 1 (1991): 49-74.

your organization selects in guiding the overall organizational culture? In a study titled, "The Value of Corporate Culture," researchers put the values of S&P 500 companies under the microscope to see if certain values were better predictors of financial performance.[105] While they found no correlation between certain values and higher financial outcomes, they did find that whether or not the employees *perceived* the management's values as authentic predicted higher financial outcomes. They also found these most common categories of values:

- *Integrity:* ethics, accountability, trust, honesty, responsibility, fairness, doing the right thing, transparency, ownership
- *Teamwork:* collaboration, cooperation
- *Innovation:* creativity, excellence, improvement, passion, pride, leadership, growth, performance, efficiency, results
- *Respect:* diversity, inclusion, development, talent, employees, dignity, empowerment
- *Quality*: customer, meeting needs, commitment, making a difference, dedication, value, exceeding expectations
- *Safety*: health, work/life balance, flexibility
- *Community*: environment, caring, citizenship
- *Communication:* openness
- *Hard Work:* reward, fun, energy

Integrity was the leading value, and was listed by almost 52 percent of the companies.[106] To sum it up, advertised values are only as good as the culture they actually represent. If a company has the mindset that branding is external and culture is internal, it is unlikely their advertised values will represent the internal culture. This disconnect between the advertised and the authentic will adversely affect the actual culture and negatively impact both internal and external stakeholders. It will limit the ability of values to guide actions and behaviors, as they properly should.

[105] Luigi Guiso, Paola Sapienza, and Luigi Zingales, "The Value of Corporate Culture," *Chicago Booth Research Paper*, no. 13-80 (November 2013), http://economics.mit.edu/files/9721.
[106] Ibid.

How to Assess Culture

Before you can infuse your sense of purpose into the entire Tribe, it's imperative to stop and assess where you currently stand. You need to take the measure of your existing stated values. What's working? What isn't working?

The roots of your culture grow deep and they can't be manipulated. Leaders can only act as catalysts for change, they cannot be dictators of change.

Once your Tribe's assumptions have been addressed, you can start to motivate your Tribe (*motivate*, not manipulate) to reexamine and potentially change their own internal assumptions about the organization and their role within it. Broadly speaking, these assumptions include:

- Beliefs about the goals of the organization
- Beliefs about the potential for individual and organizational change
- Beliefs about the types of behaviors that are rewarded
- Beliefs about the nature of the Tribe members' relations to each other

Step 1:
Assess Your Current Status

Our first step, therefore, is to get a sense of where you're starting from and determine the current state of your culture. That's not an easy task. The culture of any organization isn't simple to understand and doesn't lend itself to measurement. Some companies fall into the trap of characterizing their culture with a combination of wishful thinking and fantastical slogans rather than attempting to genuinely attain a deeper understanding of organizational life within their Tribe. This is not the way to create authentic cultural change. It is the freeway to failure. This analysis of the "people factor" needs to happen on three levels: the individual level, the team level, and the organizational level.

All of these levels can be assessed by way of one-on-one interviews. Just how deep you dig depends on your time and resources. If you expect participants to speak freely (and if they don't, the results will be meaningless) they'll need to be guaranteed anonymity. One strategy to achieve this is to bring in a third party to conduct the interviews and analyze the responses. Or, you could employ an online survey tool (e.g., SurveyMonkey) and include open-ended questions so employees have the opportunity to comment and provide helpful insights. Now, let's look at how to conduct these interviews.

Individual Level

There are several goals at the related level to assessing your current culture at the individual level. The main goal is to understand how the organization's values and purpose align with each person's personal values and purpose. Remember: purpose inspires and values guide, so this multi-tier alignment is essential. The next goal is to understand the Tribe member's intrinsic motivators. As Jennifer Abella, Vice President, People at BW Container Systems, says, "We see people as people—not as employees. They are more than their job."[107]

So, you need to ask which activities bring them pleasure and inherent satisfaction regardless of any reward or recognition they receive for it? A better understanding of these motivators can allow leadership to make informed decisions which, in turn, can make work a much more rewarding experience for everyone. The third goal of this part of the assessment is to understand what the Tribe member loves most and finds most satisfying about their work. Who or what part of their role inspires them the most?

Starting the interview with these questions sets an excellent tone for the remainder of the discussion. Lastly, if possible, try to make the Tribe

---

[107] Jennifer Abella (Vice President, People at BW Container Systems) in communication with the author, June 2017.

members dig deep and uncover their assumptions about their own roles and goals within the organization. Are there any personal habits that individuals believe they need to start, stop, or continue to align with the goals of the organization?

Team Level

The goal at the team level assessment is to understand how the culture and values influence employee interaction by asking questions such as:

- How does culture shape how teams manage strategic goals, responsibilities, and accountability?
- Are there any unintended consequences or impacts of certain values on working relationships and team functioning?

Organizational Level

The goal of this final assessment dimension is to understand how the Tribe member views the overall culture of your organization.

- What areas for improvement to the current culture do they see?
- Are the company's existing purpose and values memorable?
- Can they actually recall what they are?
- What does each value mean to the Tribe member?

You must also learn how the Tribe views the leadership through questions such as:

- How does leadership authority manifest through formal practices and informal interactions?
- How is success rewarded and how is failure addressed?
- Do you think leadership lives by the currently stated values of the organization?
- Which values or motivations truly guide the leadership's actions?

The primary benefit of conducting these interviews will be that you gain a complete and authentic understanding of the current state of your culture.

There is, of course, an amazing secondary benefit. By having the Tribe focus on what they love, they'll be prompted to reevaluate their work experiences and will form a greater appreciation of their roles within the Tribe. If carried out correctly, the process can affirm, empower, and encourage each Tribe member's self-efficacy.

These interviews should be used to evoke as much positivity as possible, and they usually do. It's likely that during this process these feelings spread from Tribe member to Tribe member and create collective positivity. This will ultimately reinforce closer relationships among the Tribe, in addition to enabling cultural growth and evolution.

In the next section, we will discuss how to interpret the responses, evaluate the current state of your culture, and use the data to create new values or redefine your current ones to ensure they properly guide your purpose journey.

Step 2:
Evaluating the Results

So, you've gone ahead and conducted those anonymous interviews. Now, let's analyze the responses and extract the most important insights about your culture. After that, we'll dig deeper into the Tribe's assumptions about the current values and whether there is an opportunity to pivot toward new values. Through these interviews, you should now know:

- What your Tribe loves most
- Their intrinsic motivations
- Their assumptions about the organization, its leaders, and how those leaders use their authority, reward success, and manage change

To organize and summarize the critical data of these insights, we use a modified version of the popular analytical framework known as SWOT: Strengths, Weaknesses, Opportunities, and Threats.

Strengths

Strengths are the shining stars of your culture. What is the best cultural attribute of your organization? What sets your culture apart from the competition and keeps the Tribe engaged and happy? For example, your Tribe could excel at cultivating a flexible work environment, or it could excel at fostering trust and mutual respect.

Weaknesses

Weaknesses are the cultural elements you identify that prevent your organization from performing at its optimum level. They include poor communication such as lapses in feedback from leadership; misalignment among the values of individual Tribe members; and, of course, misalignment between the values of your Tribe and the stated values of the organization.

Opportunities

Opportunities refer to favorable cultural factors that an organization can use to give it an advantage. What are the potential future strengths of the organization? For example, a Tribe that embraces new challenges and responsibilities has the opportunity to help its organization accelerate adaptation of changes in culture, technology, or service.

Threats

Threats are factors that can potentially harm the organization, such as leadership's misuse or overuse of power; favoritism (or the perception of favoritism), and lack of open and honest communication within the Tribe. These are the kinds of factors that lead to a destructive culture that compromises positive qualities such as credibility, candor, and caring. Weaknesses can be strengthened and improved, but threats must be eradicated, as they affect everything from employee retention to morale and attitudes to how effectively people cooperate and collaborate with one another. Try to fill each part of this matrix with the most important themes from each of the three levels (individual, team, and organizational) of your organization.

Step 3

Assessing the Tribe's Beliefs About the Values

Analyze each of your organization's values, one at a time. For each value, assess:

- Authenticity

- Effectiveness

- Alignment

- Perceived meaning

- Memorability

Authenticity

Authenticity is of extreme importance—it's probably *the* most important quality. As discussed earlier, this factor predicted the success of S&P 500 companies much better than the presence of any advertised value.

To assess authenticity, simply measure the percentage of the Tribe that felt the leadership behaved in a manner that reflected the value. More authentic values will be visible in the interactions between leadership and all stakeholders.

Effectiveness

To assess the company's effectiveness, ask these type of questions when you meet with the Tribe:

- Does the Tribe feel that the value has the desired outcome on the Tribe's behavior and decision-making?

- Is that value effective under all circumstances, or does it depend on external factors, such as motivation or workload?

A good value should guide and inspire the Tribe unconditionally and under all circumstances, especially when the company is going through rough patches. It's at these times when the ability to fall back on strong values for support and direction makes a significant difference

Alignment

To gauge the degree of the value's alignment, you should complete the following. First, map what values guide your individual Tribe members based on the interviews. Then determine what percentage of the Tribe felt that the organization's value was aligned with their own values. Now determine the extent to which Tribe members share the same values.

Perceived Meaning

Next, assess perceived meaning by examining assumptions about how each value connects to the Tribe members' behaviors and roles within the organization. Assess:

- What percentage of the Tribe understood the intended meaning of each value?

- What day-to-day behaviors did this value promote for each Tribe member?

- What personal and interpersonal interactions does this value result in?

- What percentage of those behaviors aligns with the intended meaning of the value?

Memorability

To assess memorability, determine the percentage of the Tribe that remembered and recalled the value by name and understood the intended meaning of that value.

- Remembered and recalled the value by name and

- Understood the intended meaning of that value.

If memorability is poor, determine whether it is due to either or both of the following:

- Poor internal rollout and communication of the value and its meaning.
- Tribe-wide assumptions that the value is inauthentic or meaningless.

As we've seen, research demonstrates that workers are more satisfied and committed to their company when their values are congruent with the values of their supervisor.[108] On the other hand, poor alignment makes it harder to get your Tribe to share and execute the overall goals of the organization.

It's important to recognize whether certain values have unintended or unexpected consequences on the culture of the workplace. You don't want them to backfire. For instance, the value of flexibility can be extremely advantageous, but if it manifests itself in the form of inconsistently followed processes, it can interfere with productivity. Next, we will use these insights, and the data they provide, to determine how we can improve your current culture, and where to pivot if necessary.

Step 4
Realign and Pivot Values

Some companies start out with long lists of values just as a means of marketing themselves both to their customers and their prospective employees. But as the business develops and cultures formulate, it can become difficult for its leadership, and Tribe, to deliver on each value

---

[108] Bruce M. Meglino, Elizabeth C. Ravlin, and Cheryl L. Adkins, "A Work Values Approach to Corporate Culture: A Field Test of the Value Congruence Process and Its Relationship to Individual Outcomes," *Journal of Applied Psychology* 70, no. 3 (December 2014): 424-432, https://www.researchgate.net/publication/232548618_A_Work_Values_Approach_to_Corporate_Culture_A_Field_Test_of_the_Value_Congruence_Process_and_Its_Relationship_to_Individual_Outcomes.

(especially if it's not authentic). Changes also make it necessary for the establishment of new values that motivate the Tribe, not only to achieve new heights, but also to meet future challenges.

No company should stand still, and changing values should be integral to the successful development of any organization. It's vitally important to consider value pivots during periods of growth, restructuring, and when you hit major milestones.

So, you have interviewed the Tribe and evaluated and quantified each value along the following lines:

- Authenticity
- Effectiveness
- Alignment
- Perceived meaning
- Memorability

Now, let's determine whether you need to pivot one or more of your values.

Authenticity

You may find that a small proportion of your Tribe deems one value or another to be inauthentic, and you might be tempted to simply toss it out because it doesn't meet everyone's approval. Don't overreact. That would demonstrate a lack of integrity among the leadership. Instead, work with the leadership to determine whether their individual behaviors, and/or formal organizational processes, need to change to realign with the value.

Effectiveness

Different values may motivate each Tribe member in different ways, but if over half of your Tribe perceives a value as an ineffective motivator, or even as counterproductive, you should strongly consider changing it.

Alignment, Perceived Meaning, and Memorability

Let's talk about these three factors as a group. Remember, just proclaiming the existence of a value is not enough to change your culture. Your Tribe must remember the value, understand it, and believe it. Values have the most impact when there's widespread understanding and agreement among the Tribe on their importance and personal relevance.

You don't need 100 percent consensus or buy-in to retain a value. As long as the value is perceived to be effective, it shouldn't be thrown away just because it's not memorable, or well understood by your Tribe. More importantly, values need to resonate with the purpose that gives meaning to the daily work done by your Tribe.

Now, let's talk about that daily work.

CHAPTER 6
Habits Define

"Your net worth to the world is usually determined by what remains after your bad habits are subtracted from your good ones."
—*Benjamin Franklin, Statesman, Author, Diplomat, Scientist, Inventor*

In *The Power of Habit*, an award-winning book by *New York Times* business reporter Charles Duhigg, he relates the tale of the day in October 1987 when Paul O'Neill, as the new CEO of aluminum manufacturing giant Alcoa, took the stage before a room of investors.

O'Neill, who went on to become U.S. Treasury Secretary, stunned his audience by ignoring the subjects they wanted to know all about—revenue and profit—and instead zeroed in on worker safety and lost-time accidents. He did not feel his attention was misguided even though Alcoa's safety record already was better than most—despite its employees working with metals that heat up to 1,500 degrees and machines that can rip a man's arm off.[109]

"But it's not good enough. I intend to make Alcoa the safest company in America. I intend to go for zero injuries," declared O'Neill. And he told the astonished investors, "If you want to understand how Alcoa is doing, you need to look at our workplace safety figures."[110]

One attendee later told Duhigg he had raced to a payphone and called his top 20 clients. He urged them to sell their stock immediately, saying, "The

[109] Charles Duhigg, "How 'Keystone Habits' Transformed a Corporation," *HuffPost*, February 27, 2012, https://www.huffingtonpost.com/charles-duhigg/the-power-of-habit_b_1304550.html.
[110] Drake Baer, "How Changing One Habit Helped Quintuple Alcoa's Income," *Business Insider*, April 9, 2014, http://www.businessinsider.com/how-changing-one-habit-quintupled-alcoas-income-2014-4.

board put a crazy hippie in charge, and he's going to kill the company." The investor subsequently described that call as, "Literally the worst piece of advice I gave in my entire career."[111]

That's because the altruistic emphasis on safety led to soaring profits. O'Neill instituted a better habit loop at Alcoa.

Whenever there was an injury, the unit president was required to provide O'Neill with an injury report within 24 hours, along with an action plan to prevent it from happening again. Promotion was dependent on compliance. For a unit president to meet the 24-hour deadline, she needed to hear about the injury from her VP as soon as it happened. The VP had to be in constant communication with the floor managers, and the floor managers had to rely on the workers for safety suggestions so they would have an answer for the VP when he asked for a plan. As these patterns shifted to meet the safety requirements, other aspects of the company also began to change. Better safety quickly translated into increased quality and efficiency.[112]

During O'Neill's time at Alcoa, the number of work days lost because of injury fell from 1.86 days per 100 workers to 0.2, and by 2012, the rate had fallen to 0.125. [113]Alcoa was living its values. But that impact extended beyond worker safety. One year after O'Neill's speech and refocusing the company on purpose, values, and specific habits, the company's profits hit a record high. [114]

Through one critical metric, or what Duhigg refers to as a "keystone habit," created a change that rippled through the whole culture. Duhigg says the focus on worker safety led to an examination of an inefficient manufacturing process, one that made for sub-optimal aluminum and danger to workers.

---

[111] Ibid.
[112] Dillan, "The Power of Habit Summary," *Deconstructing Excellence*, May 26, 2015, http://www. deconstructingexcellence.com/the-power-of-habit-summary/.
[113] Baer, "Alcoa's Income."
[114] Ibid.

"I knew I had to transform Alcoa. But you can't order people to change," said O'Neill. "So, I decided I was going to start by focusing on one thing. If I could start disrupting the habits around one thing, it would spread throughout the entire company."[115] That's what happened. When he retired 13 years later, Alcoa's annual net income was five times higher than when he started.

Let's fit Alcoa's transformation into our purpose-values-habits (purpose inspires, values guide, habits define) framework. By targeting zero injuries, O'Neill created a new value at Alcoa: worker safety. To support that value, he instituted several habits such as injury reporting, VP-to-floor manager communication, proactive safety plans, and worker suggestions. While he did not expressly articulate a new purpose, O'Neill's worker safety value and corresponding safety habits imply an unstated purpose: "We believe every life matters."

The new approach to safety habits led to a change in culture. The company moved the focus from profit to people, and the new goal became zero injuries. That guiding light rallied the company around this belief, and a culture of care was born. A single value gave rise to countless daily habits that transformed the company—and profits followed.

When implemented successfully, values provide a strong identity and connection between all of our stakeholders, colleagues, community, industry, and customers. They are what makes us, well, us. From the way we answer company calls to the way we handle major threats to our business, companies are responsible for countless decisions. Without predefined values, it's too easy to lean on precedent or default to personal practices to make these decisions. Our goal in this chapter is to get you in the mindset of checking in with your defined company values before every interaction and decision, and questioning old habits when necessary.

\

---

[115] Ibid.

THE SCIENCE OF STORY

How to Communicate Values Through Habits

The New Year is always an interesting time. It's when so many of us vow to change something in our lives. We're going to lose weight or exercise more, we're going to finally take the trip to Europe we've been talking about for years, or we're going to achieve a career goal. In fact, some 40 percent of us make a New Year's resolution. Now guess how many of us succeed in accomplishing that resolution. It's just eight percent.[116] You don't have to be a mathematician to work out that this means 92 percent fail.

What's the difference? What makes those individuals who comprise the eight percent successful? What helps them bridge the seemingly impossible divide between knowing what they value and living those values? The answer: their regular, day-in, day-out habits.

In 2012, habits converged with positive psychology in *The Power of Habit*. Examining neuroscience, human nature, and our seemingly limitless potential for transformation, Duhigg outlines how habits at work rewire our brains—and our lives and our companies—in the process. And he cites examples ranging from peak athletic performers like Michael Phelps, the most decorated Olympian of all time, to the excellence of the global coffee emporium, Starbucks.

We all know what it's like to have values without living them. We may well count ourselves among the New Year "resolutioners" who commit to leading healthier lives, only to fall back into greasy fast food and skipped gym sessions. The most effective way to join the eight percent who succeed in keeping resolutions is to connect the values we've identified to the habits we engage in every single day. If you want your organization to be authentic and genuine and to live its values, then specific habits that support those values must be identified, shared, and practiced within the

---

[116] "New Years Resolution Statistics," Statistic Brain, accessed November 28, 2017. https://www.statisticbrain.com/new-years-resolution-statistics/.

organization.

Steven DuPuis, for instance, cares deeply about treating everyone with equal respect, from himself to entry-level employees. "We make sure everyone has a voice," he says. "We have a very open culture." This quality helped the company make WorldBlu's "Most Democratic Workplace" list.[117] Companies earn a spot only after a rigorous "Freedom at Work" assessment process takes place.

This egalitarian mindset at DuPuis Group led to the creation of programs that make it more likely that each employee feels valued. Steven says, "Our offices have yoga every Friday, and we bring in guest speakers, from nutritionists to local farmers. We want to constantly learn and be inspired. Every quarter we also put on what we call a Campfire Event, fashioned after the French Salons of the 1800s. Campfire brings together intellectuals, artists, writers, scientists, dreamers, entrepreneurs, and inventors—those who enjoy living outside the lines. Together, over dinner, we share and connect with fresh ideas."[118]

These are the decisions, situations, and interactions that matter most, show our true colors, and show the world who we are and what our brand and company culture stands for. As we look at the business situations of how we live our values and honor our brand, we have broken down the segments or vectors of the organizational system under which most businesses operate.

Cultural Rituals/Traditions

These are the quirky little recurring practices that communicate a core value at your company and hopefully provide a sense of belonging. A 5 to 8 p.m. sprint (with pizza!) might communicate the value of hard work, while a morning group meditation reaffirms the importance of caring for

---

[117] "The 2010 WorldBlu List," Awardee Profile, WorldBlu, http://www.worldblu.com/awardee-profiles/.

[118] Steven DuPuis (Founder of DuPuis Group) in discussion with the author, July 2016.

your mind (or being), a topic more thoughtfully fleshed out in Appendix A.

In an article titled, "Want to Strengthen Workplace Culture? Design a Ritual," IDEO Organizational Design expert Mollie West and Senior Strategist at SYPartners Kate McCoubrey Judson wrote:

> Picture this: you're an engineer at Facebook's headquarters in Menlo Park. You're sitting in a lecture with a guest speaker, learning about the latest and greatest in nanotechnology. Next to you, one of your friends is capturing the speaker's best quotes on his phone. He texts a quote to a graphic designer friend who's sitting across campus in Facebook's internal print shop. The designer immediately designs a poster based on the quote, then pins them up around campus. As you walk out of the lecture, you see the posters—echoing the lecture that ended just seconds ago—already plastered on walls.
>
> Mind blown, right? But this is just another day at Facebook. The rapid poster-printing phenomenon is coordinated through Facebook's Analog Research Lab, an internal workshop open to everyone on campus. Employees can create any posters they want, on any topic they care about, and put them up anywhere—guerilla style.[119]

We were pleasantly surprised when a few of the companies we interviewed had already realized the impact of their corporate culture not only on their Tribe, but also on their Tribe's first and foremost Tribe: their families. They were so much aware of this that already they had found ways to engage them.

One story in particular really struck home. It came from Ganeden Inc., an international probiotic ingredient supplier. They took the unusual step of inviting Tribe members' parents and families to their annual holiday party so they could experience the corporate culture.Some 140 people showed up for the party, which, considering the company has 30 employees, indicates how much the gesture was appreciated. All were able

---

[119] Mollie West and Kate McCoubrey Judson, "Want to Strengthen Workplace Culture? Design a Ritual," *HuffPost*, December 6, 2017, https://www.huffingtonpost.com/great-work-cultures/want-to-strengthen-workpl_b_11730914.html.

to experience the company's gratitude and recognition. As President and CEO Michael Bush says, "When you're a kid and you do a good job, people tell your parents, but when you're an adult it's not often that your parents receive the recognition of their children's continued success."[120]

Meanwhile, the Mabbly Tribe has a handshake that inducts new members into the pack, and a Tribesgiving, where everyone cooks different parts of the meal and sits down to share what we are most thankful for. We combine our obsession with excellence and creativity by going for walking meetings to discuss personal development with individual members of the Tribe. The reason our interview process takes three months to go through— including completing an assignment—is that not everyone is a good fit for our particular culture, or our particular values. Our values shake up the way we do things, and you have to be OK with that. More on how to hire good people to come.

Sometimes rituals are created less intentionally and reveal…less than pleasant values. In 2015, the *New York Times* published an exposé of Amazon's hostile work environment, and mentioned one such troubling ritual: "The internal phone directory instructs colleagues on how to send secret feedback to one another's bosses. Employees say it is frequently used to sabotage others." The tool offers sample texts, including this: "I felt concerned about his inflexibility and openly complaining about minor tasks."[121]

Education/Training

Deloitte found that Millennials covet training and development above any other job benefits including flexible working hours, cash bonuses, free

[120] Michael Bush (President and CEO of Ganeden Inc.) in discussion with the author, July 2017.

[121] Jodi Kantor and David Streitfeld, "Inside Amazon: Wrestling Big Ideas in a Bruising Workplace," *The New York Times*, August 15, 2015, https://www.nytimes.com/2015/08/16/technology/inside-amazon-wrestling-big-ideas-in-a-bruising-workplace.html.

private healthcare, retirement funding, and greater vacation allowances.[122] Career development used to mean upward progression; now, it means growth through new experiences.[123] Far from boring employees, learning initiatives help calm our fears about our skills being rendered obsolete in the coming jobpocalypse. They help us meet personal goals, flood us with endorphins when we grasp difficult concepts, and help us re-imagine our jobs as places where we're as valued as the customers are.

After Starbucks announced that they'd be providing a four-year tuition at Arizona State's online university to their employees at no cost in 2014, applications shot up by 600,000 the following year (from 5.8 million in the 2014 fiscal year to 6.4 million in the following fiscal year).[124] "Did Starbucks Just Create The Most Epic $250 Million Recruiting Tool Ever?" a 2015 *Forbes* article wondered aloud.[125]

Employers can offer three different types of programs: personal, professional, and organizational development.

Personal Development

Personal growth is a natural extension of the human journey (after all, at the top of Maslow's Hierarchy of Needs is Self-Actualization). If we don't facilitate it, if we don't give it importance, we fail to deliver on our promise.

Set aside business metrics for a second. What do 21st Century humans need to thrive in the workplace? Emotional intelligence? Fluency in big data and artificial intelligence (often an area where traditional college

---

[122] Niall McCarthy, "Which Work Benefits Do Millennials Value Most? [Infographic]," *Forbes*, November 12, 2015, https://www.forbes.com/sites/niallmccarthy/2015/11/12/which-work-benefits-do-millennials-value-most-infographic/#2b90c03b34ff.

[123] Josh Bersin, "Learning Management Systems: Are They Coming To An End?" Deloitte, January 2017, accessed November 28, 2017, https://www.edcast.com/corp/wp-content/uploads/2017/01/2017_01_LMS_EDCAST_2.1c.pdf.

[124] Micah Solomon. "Did Starbucks Just Create the Most Epic $250 Million Recruiting Tool Ever?" *Forbes*, October 26, 2015. https://www.forbes.com/sites/micahsolomon/2015/10/24/did-starbucks-just-create-the-most-epic-250-million-recruitment-tool-ever/#4e9e804f7a5d.

[125] Ibid.

curricula lag)? One of the reasons Pixar University was founded was to sharpen their employees' creativity. "We saw how the formula crept in," said Pixar University Dean Randy Nelson. "Everyone here loves the old Disney favorites, but we never want to do one of those movies where the audience can figure out there must be a song coming here or 'He's an orphan, so he's going to have a fat little buddy.'"[126]

Professional Development

Employees want to hear their managers say, "Let's help you become a knowledge expert. Let's go deep into your functional area." "McDonald's Hamburger University can be harder to get into than Harvard and is even cooler than you'd imagine," read a recent *Business Insider* headline.[127] Long before there were 4,000 corporate universities, the threshold we passed in 2011, there was just one, and it was founded in the basement of a McDonald's in 1961.

Today, the one-week intensive program boasts over 275,000 graduates from its multiple campuses around the world. Though there are decorative grills in the building, flipping patties is not on the curriculum. "Hamburger University focuses more on leadership development, business growth, and operations procedures, with a special emphasis on service, quality, and cleanliness to help prepare students for managerial positions in the restaurant industry, " the article explained.[128] Helping employees move up within their current industry not only shows them you care about their growth, but seasons your workplace with knowledge and morale.

---

[126] Jessi Hempel, "Pixar University: Thinking Outside The Mouse," *SFGate*, June 4, 2003, http://www. sfgate.com/news/article/Pixar-University-Thinking-Outside-The-Mouse-2611923.php.

[127] Natalie Walters, "McDonald's Hamburger University can be harder to get into than Harvard and is even cooler than you'd imagine," *Business Insider*, October 24, 2015, http://www.businessinsider. com/mcdonalds-hamburger-university-2333/#hamburger-university-has-16-full-time-college-professors-on-staff-in-the-us-with-the-ability-to-teach-in-28-languages-6.

[128] Ibid.

Organizational Development

Say you've just spent substantial resources to find top talent aligned with your purpose and values. Let's look at two drastically different examples of the onboarding process:

1. Here is your 50-page manual. Let's make sure you are here 9 to 5.
2. Leaders spend time with the new hire discussing purpose and values. If it's important, shouldn't that be discussed on the level with job responsibilities? Intentional effort is given to help the new hire feel a part of the team and organization. There is a conscious effort around their successful first step that allows them to feel a part of something greater.

Which approach more likely would engage and inspire a new hire and positively reflect values in action? Most definitely the second. At Mabbly, we make sure to operationalize purpose and values through continued learning and support. When we welcome anyone into our Tribe, we share stories of the people who have lived those values and provide context to our roles of how we support the purpose of the organization. To do any less, and move forward with this book, would make us no different than the companies that employees are revolting against and departing in droves.

And so we share stories around the highs and lows of our careers, including some of those covered in our "Meet the Guys" section. As a result, Tribe members understand the driving force behind the creation of our firm and the reason we do the things we do (and avoid other practices like the plague). The end result is a surprisingly good level of engagement and retention for a young agency. You will read more about the process, mechanics, and content of storytelling in Chapter 8.

A final word: the $300-billion global training and development industry is broken. We have heard this from a number of companies as well as training and development consultants. According to *Harvard Business Review*, "American companies spend enormous amounts of money on employee training and education—$160 billion in the United States and close to $356 billion globally in 2015 alone—but they are not getting a good return on their investment. For the most part, the learning doesn't lead to better organizational performance, because people soon revert to their old ways of doing things."[129]

The problem, one of the article's authors discovered, "Was that even well-trained and motivated employees could not apply their new knowledge and skills when they returned to their units, which were entrenched in established ways of doing things. In short, the individuals had less power to change the system surrounding them than that system had to shape them."[130]

Another reason that initiatives fail is that we expect employees to absorb hours of gruesomely boring content from a dinosaur LMS (Learning Management System) and then apply it. How could they? Our minds are molded by advanced technology led by social media. Many companies are leaning into "micro-learning," which offers support for "I need help now," not "I want to learn something now." Ideally, it's a single topic or problem-based, and is rated based on helpfulness. Both micro and macro-learning have their place in a company that truly empowers their employees to make change.

Information/Communication

Transparency doesn't have to be one of your core values for you to care about your culture of communication. Liz Ryan, founder and CEO of Human Workplace, a global movement to reinvent work for people, worries about offices where, "The informal grapevine is many times more effective as a communications network than any type of official company communication."[131] In too many companies, the default setting is, 'We

---

[129] Michael Beer, Magnus Finnström, and Derek Schrader, "Why Leadership Training Fails - and What to Do about It," *Harvard Business Review*, October 2016, https://hbr.org/2016/10/why-leadership-training-fails-and-what-to-do-about-it.
[130] Ibid.
[131] Liz Ryan, "Ten Unmistakable Signs of a Toxic Culture," *Forbes*, October 20, 2016, https://www.forbes.com/sites/lizryan/2016/10/19/ten-unmistakable-signs-of-a-toxic-culture/2/#53da11297e42.

THE SCIENCE OF STORY

don't trust our people, we know better,' and information is dispersed on a need-to-know basis—or just as bad, only positive information is shared, while creating total distrust.

Dr. Michelle Rozen, author of *How to Build a Winning Company Culture*, asks every leader these four questions: "Do people in your company feel heard? Are leaders within the company open to new ideas? Is it acceptable for everyone within the company to come up with ideas, no matter what their position is? Is management transparent, open, and honest with all employees?"[132]

It's worth taking a long, hard look at personal and organizational communication. Interpersonal communication requires EQ, or emotional intelligence. Are we mindful toward each other as humans? Organizational communication requires both good processes and generosity. Are we keeping trade secrets or siloing information at the top? How do we communicate from shareholder to associate? What is our knowledge around products and services?

One company that's making it easier to become a knowledge expert is Slack, the online chat tool for teams. One self-described Gen X-er fell in love with Slack, and shares some of the top reasons why in her own words:

1. **Slack Organizes Communications in Channels.** Email is organized by time, though you can search and sort by date, subject line, sender, etc. Slack is organized by channels that you create. Think folders, but hella smarter, faster, flexible, and team-friendly.

2. **Slack Captures Institutional Knowledge.** Imagine starting a new gig and having a searchable window into the institutional knowledge and team conversations for your new project. Just dive into the channel, or search across channels, to unearth decision-making, brainstorms, documentation, and thought processes. Who

---

[132] Dr. Michelle Rozen, "How to Create a Company Culture of Communication," *HuffPost*, July 18, 2016, https://www.huffingtonpost.com/michelle-rozen/how-to-create-a-company-c_b_11055992.html.

worked on that graphic last time? Look in Slack. Why did we decide to launch the match on this day? Look in Slack.

3. **Slack Encourages Communications Across Silos.** While the bulk of my work in Slack is done in project-based channels, I truly enjoy pulling in people across the spectrum to handle a private, quick task. Try doing this by phone, email or text—it's super slow, or it just doesn't happen.[133]

Now, excessive private messaging, emoji-trading, and FOMO distracting employees en masse have burned some companies. Like all technology, it's only as good as your relationship with it. But no one can deny that when used properly, Slack accomplishes noble objectives and positively drives information exchange and communication flow.

Hiring/Reward Systems

We believe in changing the world! Now, everyone, let's focus on EBITDA of 15 percent. Let's start and end every meeting with it. All comp's around 15 percent EBITDA. Let's put "PURPOSE" and "VALUES" nice and big as a decoration on every wall. But let's hire and reward those who can help us meet 15 percent EBITDA.

This is not a parody. The financial news site *TheStreet* wrote of the fashion retailer Dillards: "Morale at this department store chain seems weighed by fears of not meeting sales targets, which threaten pay cuts."[134] One Glassdoor review complained : "The pay starts off decent but when you don't meet your sales goals you can get a pay cut or fired," and, "I can't imagine working there for so long to get pay cut after."[135]

There are other ways leadership can clue in prospective employees to

---

[133] Kerri Karvetski, "7 Reasons Why This Gen X Nonprofit Marketer Has Fallen in Love with Slack," *Kivi's Nonprofit Communications Blog*, June 15, 2017, http://www.nonprofitmarketingguide.com/blog/2017/06/15/7-reasons-why-this-gen-x-nonprofit-marketer-has-fallen-in-love-with-slack/.

[134] Rebecca McClay, "Think Amazon's Bad? Here are 6 Companies with Worse Culture," *TheStreet*, August 17, 2015, https://www.thestreet.com/story/13257755/1/6-companies-with-worse-workplaces-than-amazon.html.

[135] Ibid.

how little they care: failing to post a detailed job description explaining what success looks like or not scheduling an interview with a prospective employee's direct manager. Hiring interactions shed light on your culture, which reflects your brand. What messages do you send potential recruits?

At Mabbly, our approach can be a bit irreverent. For example, we send a dog whistle to fellow goofballs through our job descriptions. In a recent posting for a senior strategy consultant, the header read: "If You're Offered a Seat on a Rocket Ship, You Don't Ask What Seat. You Just Get On." Then, after explaining who Mabbly is, we try to understand applicants as people:

> Are you looking to put your wealth of unique experiences to the test? Are you a management consultant stuck in a deeply depressing corporate office feeling uninspired? Or do you have all the skills of a business unit leader and just don't want to wait five more years to have an opportunity lined with political minutia? Are you ready to work at a company culture that can be a reflection of you? If yes, to any of these, let's have a conversation.

We're a digital branding agency. We don't have to sound dry and droll.

It's also important for Mabbly to say that imperfection is OK as long as passion is there. Our job postings also declare: "We aren't perfect and don't expect you to be either." In the history of Mabbly, no one is really prepared for the day-to-day and there are not many organizations that have the breadth of skill sets we use every day. So, this requires a high level of inspiration and self-education to be a part of our growing Tribe.

We'll spare you a long lecture about the importance of rewarding good behavior. Anyone who's been a parent, or spent any amount of time on this earth, knows that humans thrive on praise. Make sure you spend time celebrating the win of a big client or consistently delivering on expectations that align with company purpose and show the values in action, rather than dwelling on small infractions. The recognition does not have to be major in scope, nor does it even need to be monetary. A handwritten thank-you note or a positive call-out at Tribe meeting can communicate caring and appreciation most effectively.

Policy/Authority

Some organizational systems are designed to prevent crime. Some are designed to inspire our best selves. The truth is most organizations adopt Industrial Age operating systems. We haven't changed the way we work in over 100 years. And the old, hierarchical models are failing us. They can't sustain a culture of bottom-up innovation.

Aaron Dignan, founder of the organizational design firm The Ready, believes that today's most disruptive and purposeful companies are experimenting with roles, teams, and authority, and that the three most effective approaches are Holacracy, Agile Squads, and Self Organizing. While the three systems are different in many specifics, their underlying principles are similar. Their goal is to remove politics and power from the workplace and to give employees the authority to do whatever makes sense to get their jobs done.[136]

One principle or theme the three systems share is decentralized authority. There's often a create-your-own job element—roles and employees are not one-to-one. Jean Hsu, a former Medium employee, loved what they called Dynamic Roles. She said, "This has empowered me to dynamically change the overall composition of my work at Medium over the course of almost four years. I started off as an 'Engineer,' and stepped in and out of occasional 'Project Lead' roles. Last year, I spent some time filling organizationally important roles for 'Engineering Onboarding,' and I took on a more permanent 'Group Lead' role, which maps roughly to the people management aspects of an Engineering Manager."[137] Dignan further

---

[136] Aaron Dignan, "The Last Re-Org You'll Ever Do," *Medium*, December 15, 2013, https://medium.com/the-ready/the-last-re-org-youll-ever-do-f19160f61500.

[137] Erik Van Mechelen, "3 Reasons Holacracy Didn't Work for Medium: A Perspective from Octalysis Design," *Yu-kai Chou: Gamification & Behavioral Design*, February 2, 2017, http://yukaichou.com/workplace-gamification/3-reasons-holacracy-didnt-work-for-medium-a-perspective-from-octalysis-design/.

explains that, "Holacracy achieves these goals through meetings that are specially designed to turn ideas/problems into roles, accountabilities, and policies—all of which promote 'safe to try' next steps, projects, and actions."[138]

Holacracy isn't for everyone. It's famous for being tried and abandoned, by Medium. Many have hypothesized that Medium wasn't ready to make the transition, and that companies who've given the experiment adequate time have ended up thriving. You may find yourself in the latter group.

At Spotify, which adopted the Agile/Lean methodology, employees form teams horizontally around products, not vertically around disciplines (like accounting). "Autonomy," said Henrik Kniberg, one of their coaches, "is one of our guiding principles. We aim for independent squads that can each build and release products on their own without having to be tightly coordinated in a big Agile framework. We try to avoid big projects altogether (when we can), and thereby minimize the need to coordinate work across many squads."[139]

Self-organizing companies, such as Valve and Github, take the principle of autonomy even further: "Employees are encouraged to work on whatever they want—to find the projects that engage them and do the best work of their lives."[140]

Ask yourself these questions: When your industry is disrupted, how will your employees react? Will they respond, learn quickly, and adapt gracefully? Will their autopilots remember their values? Or will they sit at their desk waiting for you to tell them what to do? If you want to keep pace with technological chance, you have to look bureaucracy squarely in the face and adopt new ways of working that celebrate participation, agility, and adaptivity. The systems discussed above could show you the way.

---

[138] Ibid.

[139] Todd Charron, "Scaling Agile at Spotify: An Interview with Henrik Kniberg," *InfoQ*, April 9, 2013, https://www.infoq.com/news/2013/04/scaling-agile-spotify-kniberg.

[140] Chris Dannen, "Inside GitHub's Super-Lean Management Strategy-And How It Drives Innovation," *Fast Company*, October 18, 2013, https://www.fastcompany.com/3020181/inside-githubs-super-lean-management-strategy-and-how-it-drives-innovation.

Response to Crises/Mistakes

It wasn't Malaysia Airlines' fault that Flight MH370 tragically disappeared in 2014. But it was their fault that they waited nearly 13 hours after losing contact with the plane before holding a press conference. And it was reprehensible to notify next of kin via a text message to assume beyond doubt that there were no survivors.[141]

We all have crises of varying degrees. Revenue drops. Legal challenges. Lawsuits. Bad Glassdoor reviews. In those moments, the raw DNA of the company makes itself known. There is no hiding. Unfortunately, in the face of real adversity, most cultures of today show the disparity between advertised values and true organizational essence. Blame is unleashed. Spinning goes into full steam.

In 1982, seven people died mysteriously after taking extra-strength TYLENOL.[142] Police soon realized that someone had laced the bottles with potassium cyanide; Johnson & Johnson, horrified, acted fast.[143] They pulled $100 million worth of TYLENOL off the shelves and even ceased advertising or producing the product. Meanwhile, they offered a $100,000 reward for anyone who found the killer, allying themselves with the efforts of the FBI.[144]

When TYLENOL came back on the market, the bottles had new tamper-resistant packaging. Knowing they still had an uphill battle to regaining their customers' trust, they also offered $2.50-off coupons. The media around the terrible incident didn't downplay the nastiness of the affair, but TYLENOL wasn't blamed. And their brand moved on.[145]

---

[141] Pamela Engel, "Here's The Text Message Malaysia Airlines Sent To The Families Of The Lost Passengers," *Business Insider*, March 24, 2014, http://www.businessinsider.com/malaysia-airlines-text-message-to-families-2014-3.

[142] Dr. Howard Markel, "How the Tylenol murders of 1982 changed the way we consume medication," *PBS News Hour*, September 29, 2014, https://www.pbs.org/newshour/health/tylenol-murders-1982.

[143] Ibid.

[144] Thomas Moore, "The fight to save Tylenol (Fortune, 1982)," *Fortune*, October 7, 2012, http://fortune.com/2012/10/07/the-fight-to-save-tylenol-fortune-1982/.

[145] Markel, "Tylenol Murders."

Transforming your culture in any of the ways above is difficult. Here are 11 key points to always bear in mind as you continue this life-changing journey.

1. Change will be incremental, but worth it. Deeply entrenched cultures change slowly over time. If you work with and within the current culture, the overall change effort will be far less jarring for your internal stakeholders.

2. All transformations should be built on existing strengths. Rather than dwelling on the weak points of your culture and focusing all your resources on attacking the negatives, make the most of the positive forces that already exist inside your Tribe.

3. Make a list of Tribe members whose actions are aligned with your ideal values and culture. Individuals who have already gotten the message and are already living the values should be empowered and enlisted to cultivate positive habits and engagement among the rest of your Tribe. They could be potential fellow purpose champions.

4. Change actions at the organizational level and the assumptions will follow. At the organizational level, some companies pursue making actionable changes in the following areas:

- Empowering employees by reducing the number of approvals needed to make decisions.

- Enhancing collaboration by setting up easy ways to facilitate joint projects.

- Strengthening interpersonal relations by formulating mutually respectful practices for addressing issues among Tribe members.

5. Change actions at the individual level turning them into keystone habits. Keystone habits are small actions that can have big implications beyond the immediate results of the initial behavior.

- For example: if your Tribe lived by the value of "Service," what habits would they exhibit for treating customers?

- If your Tribe lived by the value of "Openness," what habits would they show for proposing new ideas or feedback to one another?

6. Focus on a few critical behaviors at a time.

- Look for behaviors that are both measurable and directly related to your ideal values.

- Find behaviors that can be enacted by the greatest number of Tribe members in the shortest time.

- Start endorsing these behaviors to select groups within your Tribe who you think are most likely to spread the word to everyone else.

7. Change starts from the top. Changing culture must involve changing:

- What leaders pay attention to.

- What they measure and control.

- How they allocate resources, reward, and promote.

- The degree to which their words match their deeds.

- How they react under pressure or when things go wrong.

Top-down and bottom-up strategies won't work by themselves. You need both.

8. Build bottom-up grassroots support. Bottom-up, or grassroots, support for your change initiative is essential. And to get that you need to educate and reward your Tribe in a manner that builds appreciation for your values. Make sure to formally convey the following justifications for your cultural initiatives:

- The business reasons for the change.

- How the Tribe inspired these changes.

- How the Tribe will benefit and why they should participate.

- How the changes will take place.

- How the Tribe will be supported through the changes (e.g., training).

- Who the Tribe can go to for more information or support.

9. Infuse your values into your strategy by aligning cultural and performance goals. To be most impactful, your values must be integrated into every one of your Tribe's processes—hiring, performance appraisals, promotions, incentives, and even dismissal. Values must be infused into the "what," "how," and "why" that guide everyday behavior.

- The What:
    - Job descriptions
    - Responsibilities
    - Objectives
- The How:
    - Processes and systems
    - Standard operating procedures
- The Why:
    - The purpose behind the "what" and the "how"
    - The personal meaning that they should derive from their actions

10. Don't underestimate informal interventions. Changing formalized processes such as training and incentive structures is important, but will only go so far. Informal interventions get consequential results. For example:

- Encouraging leaders to model critical behaviors.
- Creating meaningful interactions between tribe and leadership.
- Facilitating inter-organizational social networks and interactions.

The full power of informal interventions can be harnessed by deploying informal culture leaders to spread your actionable values through everyday interactions. These leaders will influence your Tribe by modeling valued behavior and habits. Try to identify various kinds of leaders to fill the unique roles within your change initiative:

- *Motivation experts*: to be catalysts for other Tribe members' personal development

- *Role models*: to enact ideal behaviors to the rest of the Tribe

- *Networkers*: to spread your culture to all departments and groups

- *Culture captains*: to lead the way on new initiatives and technologies that transform culture

11. Track progress against measurable objectives. All the behavioral changes you aim to implement should be clearly defined as:

- Tangible

- Actionable

- Repeatable

- Observable

- Measurable

The Tribe must not only understand the purpose for the change, but also the exact behaviors and habits that they must adopt to fulfill their roles within the ideal culture.

Top firms have devised performance indicators to track cultural advancement. Some have gone so far as to create objectives and key results (OKRs) listing specific individual goals to promote development, ownership, and shared pride in cultural change. The best OKRs connect each individual action to the deeper purpose that drives the organization forward.

Let's recap. We've given you the framework: Purpose inspires. Values guide. Habits define. You understand the importance of corporate habits in living out values and purpose, and how they can affect the bottom line. You now have some tips and tricks to cultivate your organization's own purpose, values, and habits. Have we really totally covered the waterfront? Not quite. You see, during our research, it was easy for most business leaders to embrace the purpose/values/habits framework, until we asked the next natural question: How do you bring values to life? In response, the majority proclaimed (coldly), "We have our values on the website and on our walls. Our charismatic leaders talk about them annually. We are good…We live our values. We ask our employees to do what's right. That's living integrity, isn't it?"

In contrast, leaders at progressive companies became super excited to share their rituals and behaviors to make their values actionable. But they would almost always ask, "What's next? How do we really bring them to life?" That pointed our research toward positive psychology, neuroscience and personal growth, which we cover in the next chapter, "The Science of Story."

CHAPTER 7
The Science of Story

"No, no! The adventures first, explanations take such a dreadful time."
—Lewis Carrol, Author

Employees are much more motivated by their organization's transcendent purpose—*how it improves lives*—than its transactional purpose—*how it sells its goods and services*. And transcendent purpose is largely and most effectively transmitted through stories.

Take this story of a company's founding: June 5, 1968. Twelve-year-old Arnette Heintze takes a break from his lawn-mowing duties. As he walks into his house, he hears a newsflash on the radio. In the race for the presidency, Senator Robert Kennedy, winner of the California Democratic primary, has been shot following a victory speech to supporters in the ballroom of a Los Angeles hotel. Kennedy, it turns out, has been mortally wounded, felled by an assassin's bullets, like his brother before him.

Arnette hears reports of Secret Service agents being assigned for the first time to protect all Presidential candidates. He's stunned by the attack on Kennedy and intrigued by the concept of the Secret Service. He grabs an encyclopedia to read up on this "mysterious" federal agency and the brave men and women who serve...people who, he thinks, "Protect what matters."

The assassination of Bobby Kennedy and the Secret Service response has an impact—a lasting impact—on young Arnette. So lasting, in fact, that, as an adult, he enters the Secret Service. In an illustrious career, he captures a serial killer, saves a life during a shopping mall shootout, and has the honor of serving on the presidential detail protecting Presidents Bush and Clinton and their First Ladies.

Arnette parlays his years of success with the Secret Service and continues the, "Protect what matters" ethos into the corporate world, co-founding Hillard Heintze, a globally recognized strategic security and investigations firm. Under his leadership, Hillard Heintze has emerged as one of the fastest-growing private companies in the U.S., on the *Inc. 500/5000* list three years in a row, and with a rich client list, a "Who's Who" of Fortune-ranked corporations.

The impact of the assassination of a presidential candidate changed the course of Arnette's life. Today, he takes, "Protect what matters" as his corporate purpose to safeguard individuals, their loved ones, and their businesses around the globe—both personally and financially.[146]

Imagine the story of Hillard Heintze's founding being told by a recruiter in a room full of college grads, or by an HR rep in a room full of new employees. Either group would be leaning forward in rapt attention. Inspire your Tribe why they should care deeply about the work. They need to understand how it might change the world or improve lives. How will people feel when it is complete? These are the components that make information persuasive and storytelling memorable.

Don't worry if the story of your company's founding doesn't involve to-the-death shootouts. What's most important is that the story helps us understand what inspired the founder to start the company and what he/she risked in service of the greater good.

Long appreciated as an important element of marketing, storytelling is just as important for communicating your purpose internally. That's a foundational step before you can externally communicate your purpose, which we will explore later . Stories, especially authentic, compelling stories, can enhance individual performance and enhance corporate

---

[146] Arnette Heintze (Co-Founder and Chief Executive Officer at Arnette Heintze) in discussion with the author, April 2017.

performance—a statement for which we will provide brain-based scientific substantiation. Therefore, your story needs to reflect your Why—your purpose, first to your Tribe and then to the wider world.

As Grace Zuncic, Senior Vice President, Corporate Development and Strategy for Chobani, told the Korn Ferry Institute, "For any organization that wants to be purpose driven, it happens through storytelling. There needs to be a broad understanding of mission and purpose, and the sacrifices and heroic actions of people who made us who we are today. The ethos of the company culture is revealed through these stories, which continue to expand over time and are written each day."[147]

The Neuroscience and Physiology of Story

The science of story has both mind and body elements that scientists are exploring and mapping, pushing boundaries, and opening new territories with the same kind of pioneering spirit that helped Lewis and Clark penetrate the American West. Our stories literally take up biological residence in our bodies, as well as neurologically in our brains, as we will soon explain.

First, let's explore the human brain (briefly!) to try and grasp its awesome potency. Within its average weight of just three pounds lies a colossus of interconnected cellular activity. Give or take a few million, our brains comprise 100 billion brain cells (that's one followed by 11 zeros). That's about the same number as the number of stars in the Milky Way and 10 times more brain cells than reside in the brains of most monkeys. Each cell links to as many as 10,000 other cells via synapses (think crossroads), where axons and dendrites connect to form approximately 500 trillion (one followed by 14 zeros) neural highways.[148]

It's an incomprehensible superhighway of frenetic activity, a whirling

---

[147] "People on a mission," Korn Ferry Institute, https://dsqapj1lakrkc.cloudfront.net/media/sidebar_downloads/Korn_Ferry_People_on_a_Mission_1219.pdf.
[148] "Scale of the Human Brain," *AI Impacts*, April 16, 2015, https://aiimpacts.org/scale-of-the-human-brain/.

dervish of never-ending action that makes us human. Our brains are perpetually being altered by every encounter and interaction in life, a phenomenon known as neuroplasticity. Put another way: think of our brains as being plastic or malleable like Play-Doh.[149] (Really!) Our brains get shaped and molded constantly. The pace of brain research, in fact, is growing at an ever-accelerating rate. The mysteries of the mind are being unveiled all the time. But what specifically does it mean when it comes to the story?

We can measure your human response to story by hooking you up to an fMRI machine (functional magnetic resonance imaging). It measures brain activity by detecting changes associated with blood flow. Here's what such imaging reveals:

The speaker speaks. Boom. Your auditory cortex springs into action.

You listen to the words. Boom.

Broca's area (which handles the recognition and coordination of words) fires up.

Boom. Wernicke's area (understanding of language) flares.[150]

One way to summarize the neuroscience is that persuasive storytelling creates an emotional response—empathy—in the mind of the recipient, or so neuroscientist Paul J. Zak, who focuses on the impact of storytelling, believes.[151] Peering into people's brains and unraveling the mysteries within is what he does for a living. He describes it as, "An amazing neural ballet in which a story line changes the activities of people's brains."[152]

A persuasive story "hacks" a neurochemical system—the oxytocin system—that stirs up empathy, motivating us to cooperate with others.

[149] Dr. Cyndi Gilbert, "Neuroplasticity: your brain is playdough," *Cyndi Gilbert Naturopathic Doctor,* July 20, 2012, http://www.cyndigilbert.ca/neuroplasticity-your-brain-is-playdough/.

[150] Carol Turkington and Joseph Harris, *The Encyclopedia of the Brain and Brain Disorders* (New York, N.Y: Facts on File, 2009).

[151] Paul J. Zak, "How Stories Change the Brain," *Greater Good Magazine,* December 17, 2013, https://greatergood.berkeley.edu/article/item/how_stories_change_brain.

[152] Paul J. Zak, "Why Your Brain Loves Good Storytelling" Harvard Business Review, October 28, 2014, https://hbr.org/2014/10/why-your-brain-loves-good-storytelling.

More than a decade ago, Zak's lab discovered that a neurochemical called oxytocin signals that it's safe to approach others. He dubbed it, "The moral molecule." If we are shown trust, or we are the beneficiaries of kindness, oxytocin is produced. But hearing about or watching emotionally resonant characters in a story can also trigger oxytocin. This is especially true in tension-laced stories, which bind our emotions even more tightly to the characters. In Zak's words, "We found that character-driven stories do consistently cause oxytocin synthesis." He continues:

> We discovered that, in order to motivate a desire to help others, a story must first sustain attention—a scarce resource in the brain—by developing tension during the narrative. If the story is able to create that tension then it is likely that attentive viewers/listeners will come to share the emotions of the characters in it, and after it ends, likely to continue mimicking the feelings and behaviors of those characters. This explains the feeling of dominance you have after James Bond saves the world, and your motivation to work out after watching the Spartans fight in 300.[153]

That's right—not only can stories guide us toward cooperation, but they can make us feel powerful, too. And, as shared earlier, telling your story the right way will lead to more productive employees, a better customer experience, and consequently, a more sustainable company in the end, which will lead to more personal and financial reward. So what are the best internal opportunities for storytelling in your company?

Tell Your Founding Story

Each company's founding story needs to be imbued into the members of its Tribe. What obstacles were overcome in getting the enterprise off the ground? What passion saved the day? How was success ultimately achieved?

---

[153] Ibid.

Take the story of how Chicago's leading real estate company got started for example. Traditionally, real estate brokers brand their business with their own names. But when Michael Golden and Thad Wong decided to open their own enterprise because of a conflict of a interest and little financing, they wanted to be anything but traditional. Besides, the name "Golden Wong" was open to all kinds of connotations and misinterpretations. And on top of that, with a genuine sense of humility, they wanted the company not to be, "All about them."

Thad explained, "We knew we wanted the company to be bigger than we are. We didn't want buyers and sellers to feel like they were 'less than' because they weren't working with Golden or Wong." So, in a stroke of marketing genius, Thad thought if he could use a common tech symbol in their name—like the '@' symbol—they would have a marketing and advertising advantage that they couldn't afford back then in the year 2000.

And just like that, @properties was born. Their unique name is truly a reflection of the choices they made that differentiated them from their competitors. When the market crashed, and many brokerages were cutting back on company perks, bonuses, and marketing efforts just to save profits, @properties did the opposite. They invested more in their people and built up a savvy in-house marketing department to boot. This allowed them to attract high-caliber agents who were looking for a place that would value them over profits and ride out the storm…together.

As Thad says, "We continually reinvest in our people whether it's through personal growth, marketing, or technology. Each individual being valued never changes, no matter if you have one employee or 1,000 employees. Unlike many companies who outsource their marketing efforts we do ours in-house so our brand is a true reflection of our culture."

To this day, their focus has not shifted from people, culture, innovation, and education. It's no surprise @properties is Chicago's #1 real estate company and one of the most recognizable local brands.[154]

---

[154] Thad Wong (Co-Founder of @properties) in discussion with the author, July 2017.

The creation myth is not just an asset just for startups. As those businesses grow into established firms and individual founders figure less prominently, the origin story can serve as both a road map and moral compass.

What if your product is, well, unglamorous? Try to isolate a circumstance in which your product or service makes all the difference. Slava Menn, the co-founder of Fortified Bicycle Alliance, a manufacturer of heavy-duty, theft-resistant bicycle lights, worried that he didn't have a powerful before-and-after story. There is nothing particularly emotional about bike lights. "It's one of the more boring products on a bike," Menn told *Inc.* magazine.[155] Then something happened. "Our friend had his bike light stolen; then he got hit by a car coming home," Menn says. "It was emotional and true and so simple that a person could retell it the same way after hearing it once."[156]

"I'm hard-pressed to think of a company that doesn't have an interesting foundational story," Paul Smith, an executive coach and former director of market research at Procter & Gamble told *Inc.* magazine. "But I suspect there are many that haven't crafted and told theirs. And they're important. People want to be part of something bigger than themselves. A nameless, faceless corporation with no real purpose, no story, is not an inspiring place to be."[157]

So craft a founding story that reminds your Tribe how their efforts map onto the values and ultimate success of your company. Connecting the dots in this way proves a key step toward engaging and galvanizing.

Share Inspiring Stories of Success — or Failure

Your Tribe will relate to stories in which they can see themselves. Content could highlight heroic contributions made by individual colleagues or the celebration of a stunning breakthrough achievement or the result of

---

[155] Adam Bluestein, "How to Tell Your Company's Story," *Inc Magazine*, February 2014, https://www.inc.com/magazine/201402/adam-bluestein/sara-blakely-how-i-got-started.html.
[156] Ibid.
[157] Ibid.

a long, collaborative process that transforms a company's identity. The best stories are told by culture captains and celebrate people getting things done in a manner that aligns with these values:

- Rewards for greatness
- Consequences of failure
- Critical events and lasting outcomes
- Heroic contributions of individual Tribe members

If told correctly, such stories provide your Tribe with direction by energizing them toward a shared goal. Stories are also the best way to transmit your culture, values, priorities, and history to *new* Tribe members. They're often the first steps in helping a new Tribe member identify with your brand, which is a reflection of your culture.

For instance, Clorox lines the walls of its offices with photos from major moments in the company's history—from wartime, to natural disasters, to the Apollo missions. During World War II, the company earned the respect of consumers when it ignored recommendations from special interest groups to dilute its powerful Clorox liquid bleach. It just couldn't bring itself to compromise the quality of the product. The company also conducted itself honorably when it declined to enforce pre-war contracts that would have spared it from price increases in raw materials.

Internally, Clorox strives hard to communicate its values throughout its 8,000-employee worldwide workforce with a key focus on transmitting the story of the company's founding culture. Chief Marketing Officer Eric Reynolds says, "We have a strong sense of history. The stories are on our walls and on our websites. We want people to know that our commitment to clean has been unerring. Succeeding for more than 100 years isn't about any one team or managers, it's about your values. That's what carries you through time."[158]

---

[158] Eric Reynolds (Chief Marketing Officer at Clorox) in communication with the author, November 2016.

Stories about pivotal moments or heroic actions from your company's history can tug at your Tribe's emotions, helping them identify with the company. Such stories also allow you to reward and recognize successes with the rest of your Tribe.

Tell Personal Stories

Vanessa Van Edwards, author of *Captivate: The Science of Succeeding with People,* suggests three different before and after narratives to capture the loyalty of listeners.[159] One route is to show how listeners themselves have benefits that they didn't have before. ("20 years after our founding, we've created hundreds of jobs...") Another is to, "Tie your 'because' to a mutual benefit, or the way something could help an entire community... Apple's "Think Different" slogan is an appeal to both the user and the world to challenge the status quo." A third option—and a surprisingly persuasive one—is to simply share your own passion for a cause with your listeners. "If something means a lot to you, or would make you incredibly happy, harness that authentic passion to create a powerful 'because.'"[160] Van Edwards mentions Mark Gordon, founder of Citizens of the World Charter Schools, as an example of someone who rallied many to his cause during the early founding days. "Gordon believes fervently in equality and diversity. He also has two young daughters whom he wants the best for. Even if those aren't your own goals, hearing him speak is powerfully moving."[161]

Or take ISACA, a rapidly accelerating not-for-profit focused partly on addressing the challenges of the next frontier: cyber security. When embarking on a purpose transformation, they brought in a new CMO, Tim Mason, a veteran marketing executive. They formed their purpose: "To help you realize the positive potential of technology," and asked Tim to

---

[159] Vanessa Van Edwards, Captivate: *The Science of Succeeding with People* (New York: Portfolio/Penguin, 2017).
[160] Ibid.
[161] Ibid.

present the organization's purpose to its 500 chapter leaders, executives and board members.

Tim knew his presentation had to truly hit home with everyone, so he decided to frame it in the context of what they do every day and help them realize that the positive potential is in the outcomes of their work. ISACA specializes in IT audit, risk, governance, and cyber security—topics that don't generally elicit positive thoughts.

Tim felt differently. He shared with his audience that when his son was serving in the military it was extremely difficult to communicate with him. However, every morning he would log on to Facebook and open his user profile. If his son's status button was green, it meant he was online. It also meant he was alive. While you can debate the virtues of Facebook, you can't debate the fact that without the professionals in the room who every day work in risk, assurance, governance, and cyber security, Facebook and other platforms could not exist. "To help you realize the positive potential of technology" now had a deeper, more impactful meaning.[162]

Instead of focusing on what they prevent, the ISACA team now talks about what they enable. Tim's personal story gave his Tribe the permission to believe in something bigger, something good. His story still gives us goosebumps. One person's story can dramatically change an entire Tribe's perspective.

The aim is to deeply understand why you exist and from there, create impact, and it then becomes a constant evolution. Momentum may begin with an individual (like Tim) and grow to fuel an organization, which then, in turn, can form a conscious choice to deliver on that purpose every day. And it's important to remember that if an organizational purpose is truly aspirational, it can literally create a change in the world.

---

[162] Tim Mason (CMO at ISACA) in discussion with the author, July 2017.

Communicate Boring Messages
Effectively, Too!

Not all workplace messages are exciting. It's also important that more routine matters, such as budgeting, process, and housekeeping meetings intentionally involve story. Forget your company's purpose for a second (blasphemy, we know!). Say you're holding a meeting to explain that Q3 profits met expectations, but just barely. It's crucial to avoid just-give-me-the-facts scenarios. You can't drive home a message armed with nothing more than facts and figures. Character-driven stories with emotional content not only result in a better understanding of a speaker's key points, but also enable better recall weeks later. Zak says, "In terms of making impact, this blows the standard PowerPoint presentation to bits."[163]

Zak advises that every presentation should start with a compelling, human-scale story. Let's say the presenter is talking about a swimming race in a harbor. He's told you there are ten contestants swimming from Point A to Point B. What then if he goes on to describe the scene—the salty smell of the seawater? Boom. The olfactory areas of your brain (the areas responsible for the sense of smell) turn on. You know that smell. You can imagine it. What then if he tells you the waves are choppy as the contestants swim freestyle and carve their way forward? Boom. Your motor cortex revs up. What if there's a major battle for first place? It's an exciting race to the finish as two swimmers go back and forth taking the lead fighting to be the winner. Boom.

Your emotional center (the limbic brain) skyrockets into high gear.

This is all happening faster than a split second. And the effect is so much greater than if the speaker simply said, "10 contestants swam across the harbor." Brain scans reveal that your brain doesn't distinguish between being an active participant in an event versus being a passive, yet

---

[163] Paul J. Zak, *Trust Factor: The Science of Creating High-Performance Companies* (New York, NY: AMACOM, 2017).

mentally involved, spectator. If the story of the swimming competition is told well, you're there, just as if you are one of the actual swimmers. Just *thinking* about swimming can fire up the same neurons as if you were really swimming. This is called grounded cognition. After pulling the listener into the swimming story, you would then, of course, link to the need perform better to the realities of marketplace competition. Even better would be if the speaker shared a relevant personal story.

We are not suggesting that facts and figures should be stripped out of a presentation to your Tribe. But when you use story on top of data, you move people emotionally, as well as intellectually. Statistics may seem uncontestable. You may believe that the facts are the facts. Or you just may tune them out. But quoting statistic after statistic forces people to think analytically, and that can provoke skepticism. Stories, on the other hand, spark emotion—and, as we have seen, real physical and chemical changes in our bodies. Integrate them wherever and whenever possible. Doing so shouldn't be a "one and done" deal.

So, we've discovered how to ignite passion within your Tribe to adopt and implement all the attributes required for a purposeful organization. But it's a driving force you can't keep locked between the four walls of your enterprise. What about the wider world? Now you come to the critical stage of Express: effectively communicating your message and beliefs to the community at large.

CHAPTER 8

Express

"Expressing your essence entirely is what we live for."
—Oscar Wilde, Poet and Playwright

We express ourselves the moment we enter this world. Usually, it's a loud, piercing cry that informs parents their newborn has moved from the silence and protection of the womb into a new environment. That initial moment of expression is real and raw. It's authentic and awesome. It's who we are. It's our true voice, our true self.

Expression is not superficial (*ex·pres·sion* — the act of making known one's thoughts or feelings).[164] We believe brand expression should be as authentic as our true selves: as unfiltered as possible. But as you've read thus far, by now you've probably realized that. We've moved from the need to hold a genuine belief in the power of purpose, to discovering your purpose, and then to igniting it within your Tribe. In this stage, Express, you announce to the world that you've arrived. It's how you communicate *externally* to let everyone know who you are and what you believe in.

Brand expression is not only an articulation of your values and purpose and a true reflection of your culture. It's the way you signal your corporate identity, reaching out and touching all stakeholders intimately and meaningfully. It's a multi-sensory way to convey your brand's core purpose and its relevance to their lives. It has impact and import.

As we said earlier, Express is *not* self-serving hype with a clever tagline designed to sell a product, price, or promotion. Instead, we're suggesting a paradigm shift: creating educational, inspirational and, most of all, authentic, digital content to engage with your audiences. To see how it's

---

[164] *English Oxford Living Dictionaries*, online ed., "expression."

done…and done well, read on for how one organization executes this stage of the process, with impact.

African lions. Arctic polar bears. Gray seals. Red pandas. Waddling penguins. Chest-thumping gorillas. The nation's only privately managed FREE admission zoo, Lincoln Park Zoo in Chicago, attracts more than 3.6 million visitors every year who are connected with nature by a full-time staff of 267 people, aided by 150 part-time/seasonal staff and more than 1,300 volunteers.

In March of 2017, after a two-year journey of discovery, the zoo announced its new vision to inspire communities to create environments where wildlife can thrive in our urbanizing world. The zoo exists, of course, to provide that free, family-oriented wildlife experience. But its purpose goes far beyond its own habitat. Amanda Willard, Vice President of Marketing and Brand at Lincoln Park Zoo, provides four examples of how they express their vision:

1. **ZooMonitor:** This is a free app developed at Lincoln Park Zoo that helps experts track and analyze animal behavior so that they can make data-driven improvements in animal care and, ultimately, welfare. More than 180 institutions worldwide have already downloaded it.

2. **Community Engagement:** Over the next five years, Lincoln Park Zoo will partner with local communities to connect people with wildlife in their own backyards—starting in Little Village on Chicago's West Side.

3. **Urban Wildlife Information Network (UWIN):** The zoo is expanding UWIN, the first scientific initiative created to study and understand urban wildlife, into cities nationwide, building on the largest set of urban wildlife data in the world and creating best practices for building wildlife-friendly cities. Eight cities have already joined.

4. **Serengeti Health Initiative:** Through this program, which

vaccinates domestic dogs in Serengeti, Tanzania, the zoo is reducing disease in both animals and humans. Wildlife surveys have identified domestic dogs as a major source of rabies and canine distemper outbreaks that have devastated the Serengeti's lion, hyena, and African wild dog populations. In fact, when the program started in 2003, there were 250 cases of rabies locally every year. Now, with some 100,000 dogs vaccinated annually, the number of rabies' cases has been cut to zero.[165]

Lincoln Park Zoo shared the rationale behind its new vision through a two-week rollout to all employees and volunteers spearheaded by Amanda, as well as the President and CEO, Kevin Bell. The rollout included messaging in a mock game show format. Externally, you can't miss the branding "For Wildlife. For All." You see it on banners near the zoo, bus shelters, online advertising, the member magazine, and employee uniforms.

Kevin Bell says, "A commitment to wildlife conservation is not, of course, new for Lincoln Park Zoo. What is new and very exciting for the organization is to create a vision that exemplifies that commitment, sharpens our focus, and drives us to share our expertise and success in a way that will have a real and positive impact on the world's wildlife."[166] And it all begins in the urban "jungle" of Chicago.

Traditionally, of course, we have thought of branding as being inside marketing. What's different now is that we believe branding is at the intersection of *purpose discovery* and marketing. Companies that succeed do so because they managed to clearly communicate their purpose—no easy task—so that others believe in their beliefs. Great leaders, who understand purpose, inspire individuals internally (ignite) and externally (express).

---

[165] Amanda Willard (Vice President of Marketing and Brand at Lincoln Park Zoo) in discussion with the author, March 2017.

[166] "Lincoln Park Zoo Unveils New National Conservation Efforts," *NBC 5 Chicago*, March 23, 2017, https://www.nbcchicago.com/news/local/Lincoln-Park-Zoo-Unveils-New-Conservation-Efforts-416984943.html.

The diagram below illustrates our overarching philosophy.

Note what's at the center: Story.

Storytelling with a Heart

Like the powerful stories passed down through generations of employees, the story you tell the world should highlight what makes you different from everybody else.

- What is your aspirational, simple, and genuine Why?
- What problem are you solving?
- Why are you passionate about solving it?
- What values does your internal culture hold dear?

Take the story that won gold in the 2015 Stevie Awards (prizes that were created to recognize business accomplishments worldwide). The story was told in a video called, "Unsung Hero," and it was made for the kind of company you don't normally expect to have heart—an insurance company. Thai Life Insurance, however, is different. You can tell that from its purpose statement: "More than just life insurance."[167]

In a saturated life insurance market, Thai Life set out to connect to potential future customers. It looked to the future by looking to the past. It felt that people in Thailand had become more materialistic and self-centered, focusing on wealth and social status as their main priority in life. In days gone by, Thai used to take care of each other and extended the courtesy of kindness to each other. How to recapture that? How to show that their company was contributing to a solution through contagious acts of kindness? How to show their brand belief in the value of life?

Thai Life created "Unsung Hero" about a man doing good. His everyday acts of kindness included helping a street vendor move her heavy cart, secretly hanging a bunch of bananas on the handle of an old lady's apartment door, giving up his seat on the bus, sharing his meal with a hungry dog, and handing over what little cash he has in his wallet to a woman and her young daughter begging on the street (genuinely, as it turns out, for the little girl's education). He did all of this. Every day.[168]

The aim of the video was to make people understand and appreciate the value of life to help others, especially the less fortunate. According to Robin Hick's article, "Unsung Hero" does just that in a powerful way, so powerful that:

- Within four weeks, it had over 17 million views from 232 countries.

- "It's the ninth most shared viral video in the world."

- The video has had over 18 million engagements.

- The impact the company's commercials have is immense. For

---

[167] "Thai LIfe Insurance - CSR Program of the Year," The International Business Awards, http://stevieawards.com/iba/thai-life-insurance-csr-program-year.
[168] Aaron Taube, "All Of Thailand Is Compulsively Weeping Over This One Life Insurance Ad," *Business Insider*, April 10, 2014, http://www.businessinsider.com/thai-life-tearjerker-ad-2014-4.

years, the company experiences at least as much growth as the category does.[169]

All of this from a commercial's three-minute story showing how a young man's everyday acts of kindness not only bring immense joy to the recipients, but also to the giver.

Also worth emulating is up-and-coming healthcare company Philips, which was ranked third in RY's "Fit for Purpose" list, and was highly applauded for its use of social media in showcasing its purpose. The firm created a video called "Breathless Choir," a highly emotive short film that tells the story of a group of people whose breathing disabilities had gotten in the way of their love of singing. Philips chronicled their journey as they learned new techniques to save breath while singing—all part of an effort to promote one of its medical devices.[170]

Sharing and Expressing *Your* Story

1. Be genuine. Auction house Christie's has many customers who sell high-value works of art and donate the proceeds to social causes that align with their personal values or passions, or those of the gifting institution. In fact, in the year 2014 alone, nonprofits benefitted to the tune of $300 million through sales put under the hammer by the auctioneers. But anything less than sincerity backfires, says Christie's Chief Corporate Social Responsibility Officer Toby Usnick.[171]

Toby told author Jeannette McMurtry, "You can't fake caring. If you pretend to care about a cause you align with, or a cause that is important to your customer, [you] won't succeed. Caring to make a

---

[169] Robin Hicks, "Why Thai Life Insurance ads are so consistently, tear-jerkingly brilliant," *Mumbrella Asia*, January 29, 2015, https://www.mumbrella.asia/2015/01/beyond-bright-shiny-things-real-issues-emerge-ces-marketers.

[170] Alexandra Bruell, "Tech Company Takes Top Prize in Cannes Pharma Category as Health Sees New Entrants," *AdAge*, June 18, 2016, http://adage.com/article/agency-news/tech-company-takes-top-prize-cannes-lions-pharma-category/304578/.

[171] Jeanette McMurtry, "The Purpose-Driven Brand," *Target Marketing*, April 16, 2015, http://www.targetmarketingmag.com/post/the-purpose-driven-brand-why-it-matters-more-than-ever/all/.

difference must be part of your culture, your drive, and your passion at all levels."[172] And if your first thought is that you're not sure that your Tribe agrees on a single thing you all care about, head back to the Discover stage!

2. Understand your audience. Engagement in story depends on how well the narrative serves the needs and goals of the audience. What does your audience want from your stories? Are they seeking to be entertained? Informed? Are they longing for a human connection? Audiences looking for information engage best with well-researched content that speaks to their interest. Those who seek to be entertained respond to engaging storylines. Audiences that seek human connection will respond to stories that allow them to identify with your brand.

3. Tell stories in the first person. First person narrative helps audiences suspend disbelief and transports them into the story. It's about giving the audience a chance to peer behind the curtain and connect at a human level with the storyteller. First person narrative is one of the reasons that blogs, usually written in the first person, have become so popular. They create a sense of identification in the audience.

4. Establish an appropriate voice. One challenge that exists in brand storytelling is choosing the right voice for your particular audience. Some individuals are more inclined to engage emotionally than others; this is called the need for affect.[173] How individuals engage with certain characters varies as well. Women, for instance, may identify with— and be more persuaded by—likeable opposite sex characters, whereas likeability is not as important to men.[174] Carefully consider what voice or character will be most appealing to your brand's audience.

---

[172] Ibid.

[173] Gregory R. Maio and Victoria M. Esses, "The need for affect: Individual differences in the motivation to approach or avoid emotions," *Journal of Personality* 69, no. 4 (2001): 583-615.

[174] Adam Fridman, "Empathy Makes Us Human - Connecting Audiences to Your Brand's Story," *Inc.*, September 28, 2016, https://www.inc.com/adam-fridman/empathy-makes-us-human--connecting-audiences-to-your-brands-story.html.

5. Pay attention to quality. Quality issues such as overly complicated storylines, multiple narrators, or a lack of consistent voice can impede the development of empathy with a reader or viewer. Unreliable narrators or lack of research and fact checking can also make a brand story less empathetic. "Narrative dissonance ," which is when the stories a brand tells don't align with how it conducts business, can also get in the way of empathy.[175]

Communication is rapidly changing in the digital age of mobile, Facebook, VR, AI—and whatever is around the corner. So, let's look at the ways to use multiple channels most effectively. We touched on this approach—internal media hubs—in the Ignite chapter, as a means of communicating internally with our Tribe. Internal media hubs are just as important, if not more important, for us to Express our beliefs and culture externally.

How to Build a Communication and Content Strategy with Purpose: Welcome to the World of Media Hubs

Think of an internal media hub like the hub of a wheel. All the spikes that connect the hub to the rim need to be in place for a perfect ride, and the more spokes that are missing, the rockier your journey is going to be. Keep riding with missing spokes and you're going to destroy the wheel. It's the same with a media outreach campaign.

It's no longer good enough to simply have a blog. Blogs, per se, are dead. They're too one-dimensional. Not many leaders view their blogs as anything more than content needed for SEO and to show that they are, well, *alive.*

Today is the age of the brand journalist, the time for brands to share what they believe with a *multi-spoke strategy*—spokes for a digital magazine,

---

[175] Ibid.

podcast, video, blog, and, yes, a full-length book. Spokes that communicate in a myriad of diverse ways, spokes that allow for interaction, spokes that stimulate a sense of purpose and togetherness, and that make people feel part of something greater are all necessary.

In our two years of research, we've uncovered hundreds of notable examples of effective strategy execution using media hubs. Let's share a few of the most outstanding. Then we'll cover the mechanics of building a media hub to enhance external storytelling.

M Live by Marriot

Step inside the Bethesda, Maryland headquarters of Marriott International, and at first glance you think you have walked into the lobby of one of their ritzy up-market hotels, but then you spy nine large flashing screens that look like the nerve center of a major television network. You've entered the zone that's been dubbed "M Live." It's Marriott's foray into capitalizing on the rapidly changing digital landscape.[176]

Marriott's team has created a successful TV show, hit short films, a personalized online travel magazine, and even a virtual reality experience. David Beebe, Marriott's Emmy-winning Vice President of Global Creative says, "We hire a lot of media, took a lot of people who were previously storytellers, turned them into marketers. It's all the same today. You can't argue with the fact that people aren't engaging with traditional [advertising] and this is the way to do it. You have to try it."[177]

Beebe told *Contently* that they have a three-C approach: scaling content, building a community around that content, and driving commerce. To that end, they've joined forces with an eclectic array of creative talent. To build trust with customers and have content that appeals to other outlets, any Marriott branding in the content is very low-key. At the end of the day,

---

[176] Joe Lazauskas, "'We're a Media Company Now': Inside Marriott's Incredible Money-Making Content Studio," *Contently*, November 5, 2015, https://contently.com/strategist/2015/11/05/were-a-media-company-now-inside-marriotts-incredible-money-making-content-studio/.
[177] Ibid.

they know they must tell a good story. Beebe says, "That's really what our goal is. To take all the brand marketers, all the brand leaders and teams, and turn them into great storytellers."[178]

Media House by Red Bull

How did Red Bull get to be the best-selling energy drink in the world with more than five billion cans guzzled each year?[179] They took the road less traveled. Instead of pursuing a traditional approach to mass marketing, Red Bull has generated awareness and created a seductive "brand myth" by way of sponsoring extreme sports and stunts.

You name it, they do it. Surfing. Kayaking. Cliff diving. Air racing. Space diving. Motocross. There's also mountain running, mountain biking, and paragliding, among other out-there activities. Additionally, they own sports teams and a music label.[180] Red Bull is a pioneer, and to broadcast its message, the company set up its own media hub: Media House, which is now, it says, one of the world's leading media companies.[181]

Media House creates compelling content across media channels as varied as TV, mobile, digital, audio, and print. In 2017, it even launched its own virtual reality platform, which hosts an array of sport, travel, and music content designed to be viewed with a VR headset or with something like Google Cardboard. That's taking a media hub into a whole new sphere and certainly substantiates Red Bull Media House's declaration: "We're on a mission to fascinate."[182]

Margot vs. Lily by Nike

Nike is an exemplary leader in so many ways. Its latest initiative for

[178] Ibid.

[179] "Number of Red Bull cans sold worldwide from 2011 to 2016 (in billions)," *Statista*, https://www.statista.com/statistics/275163/red-bulls-number-of-cans-sold-worldwide/.

[180] Mary Zawistowski, "Red Bull - More Than Just an Energy Drink," *social2b*, https://social2b.com/red-bull-more-than-just-an-energy-drink/.

[181] Ibid.

[182] Ibid.

promoting to the female market—Millennials, in particular—is an eight-episode YouTube series called "Margot versus Lily." The two main characters are a pair of interracial, adopted sisters with opposite interests. One is a socially challenged athletic junkie; the other is an outgoing woman who doesn't really care about athletic activities. The series follows a competition between the two with product placements that have impact, but don't overwhelm.[183] We can't wait to see what Nike does next.

Fresh Food Matters by Sub-Zero

Want to buy a refrigerator? Sub-Zero takes an approach that educates and entertains consumers while subtly promoting its own brand. Its message, "Think fresh," is delivered in videos with the aid of multiple foodie influencers (and brave consumers) who allow the contents of their refrigerators to be analyzed .

Sub-Zero's #freshfoodmatters initiative involves consumers by donating $5 every time the hashtag is used.[184] The money raised goes to help kids start 25 new gardens to grow fresh food. The freshfoodmatters. com site also delivers information on foods that are in season, as well as the best way to store certain foods. And when you need to buy a refrigerator, of course, you know where to go!

The Message by GE

General Electric is one of the masters—if not *the* master—in creating a media hub. One element for us that's especially worthy of acknowledgment is GE's eight-part podcast *The Message*, which had 1.2 million downloads within eight weeks of its launch in 2016 and quickly rose to number one

---

[183] John Kell, "This Is The New Way Nike Is Going After Women," *Fortune*, January 28, 2016, http://fortune.com/2016/01/28/nike-youtube-margot-lily/.
[184] "Sub-Zero Announces Fresh Food Matters Initiative Highlighting Fresh Food's Impact, Empowering People to Choose Fresh," *Sub-Zero*, April 26, 2016, http://www.subzero-wolf.com/company/press-releases/sub-zero-announces-fresh-food-matters-initiative.

on the iTunes podcast chart.[185]

The GE Podcast Theater is a modern spin on the famous General Electric Theater of the 1950s hosted by Ronald Reagan. And *The Message*, which is all about cryptographers investigating mysterious alien transmissions, is a tribute to Orson Welles's *War of the Worlds*, blurring fiction and reality. Specifically designed for a podcast audience, it has GE technology tastefully yet unmistakably at its heart: a masterful message.[186]

The Share Space by IKEA

Real people. Real rooms. Real furniture. Real renovations. IKEA provides theshare-space.com for shoppers to showcase their remodels, both through photos and how-to articles.[187] It's a simple site, but all the more interesting because its users contribute the content: people like you. It's user-friendly for the consumer and budget-friendly for the company. And it just so happens that most of the furniture that consumers have chosen for their homes and offices come from the iconic Swedish company. Let the people do your marketing for you!

The Wink by Clinique

Clinique's founder is a former *Vogue* editor, so it was no great surprise when the company created its own online magazine, connecting consumers with the people, places, and things that inspire Clinique. The site is interactive across all social media platforms, so users can share and comment on articles much more efficiently and effectively, resulting in more shares, more clicks, more traffic, and more sales.[188]

[185] Jeff Beer, "How General Electric Created the Hit Science-Fiction Podcast 'The Message,'" *Fast Company*, November 25, 2015, https://www.fastcompany.com/3053982/how-general-electric-created-the-hit-science-fiction-podcast-the-message.
[186] David Sims, "The Radio-Age Genius of The Message," *The Atlantic*, November 21, 2015, https://www.theatlantic.com/entertainment/archive/2015/11/the-message-podcast/417051/.
[187] "IKEA Announces New 'Design by IKEA' Blog and 'Share Space' Photo-Sharing Website," *IKEA Corporate News*, August 16, 2011, http://www.ikea.com/us/en/about_ikea/newsitem/Blog_Share_Space_2011_release.
[188] SaudiBeauty, "Introducing Clinique's Editorial Platform...The Wink," SaudiBEAUTY, October 2015, http://saudibeautyblog.com/introducing-cliniques-editorial-platformthe-wink/.

Small Business Revolution by Deluxe

Small Business Revolution is a media hub that showcases the successes of small businesses across America. It was debuted by Deluxe in 2015 to celebrate a century of the company providing marketing and other services to small businesses and financial institutions. In 2016, its second year, there were 14,000 entries all vying for a $500,000 town revitalization prize. The stories of finalists were all captured on video, Facebook, Instagram, Twitter, and blogs, which is a terrific way to build relationships with small companies.[189]

How to Build Your Own Media Hub

So, you're not Red Bull, Marriott, Nike, or GE. You still can build your own media hub to get the word out about your purpose. Talk to any good salesperson and they will say, "Just get me in the room with someone." We believe this should be the sole role of marketers today—building the same kind of human relationships with digital content. Research. Engage. Educate. Inspire. Add value. In brief, here are the steps you should take:

1. Build a sales target list of companies you want to meet.

2. Identify the people inside the organizations who are of interest.

3. Use LinkedIn to data-mine their names and contact information.

4. Research a topic in which they have expertise and are looking to share with the world.

5. Rebrand your blog or build an off-site landing page with a series of articles and videos discussing a range of topics. Create a communication template for outreach with links to your media hub asking them to be featured around "topic X." Tell them you found them from a quick LinkedIn search and think they would be a good fit.

---

[189] Kate Maddox, "Deluxe Rolls Out 'Small Business Revolution' For Its Centennial," AdAge, April 21, 2015, http://adage.com/article/btob/deluxe-rolls-small-business-revolution-centennial/298174/.

6. Invite them to your "studio" where you interview them for a video or article.

7. Publish the article, video, or other multimedia piece of content.

8. Nurture an opportunity.

9. Add value and then close.

This communication and content strategy can be executed by any brand, big or small. What's important for any organization is to build human relationships with digital content from an exchange of value that is based upon shared beliefs. Through a digital media hub, people learn what to expect from the brand and the company learns what its brand must deliver to its stakeholders. The result is a richer and more compelling brand experience that stakeholders value and trust.

As your brand is a collection of expectations that others have about you, brand expression is the art and science of managing those expectations. You can have the best, most dedicated Tribe in the world who have a passionate belief in a purpose that's second-to-none, but it's all to no avail if you don't discover the best ways to communicate it to your clients and customers.

CHAPTER 9

Conscious Conclusions: Mindful and Professional Habits

*"We are what we repeatedly do. Excellence, then,
is not an act but a habit."*
—Aristotle

As we discussed earlier in the book, purpose inspires and values guide. Let's start to discuss how habits define. We have talked about the importance of meaning, tips, and stories on how to discover purpose, ignite a culture, and express our beliefs to customers and the world. Now what? To make any significant transformation, it starts with habits, conscious and unconscious. We have to be first mindful or aware of our decisions and interactions daily, and how they align with our purpose and values.

Living Values

The top value of Fortune 500 companies is integrity. When asked to explain it, the typical response was, "We ask our employees to DO the right thing." Here lies the conundrum: to DO the right thing, shouldn't the first step. Consider BEING in the right state of mind. Ever tried making the RIGHT decision during the most stressful time?

This is where mindful habits come in–for the uninitiated, a dictionary definition of mindfulness is, "A mental state achieved by focusing one's awareness on the present moment while calmly acknowledging and accepting one's feelings, thoughts, and bodily sensations used as a therapeutic technique."[190] We can see how the Starbucks "being present"

---

[190] *English Oxford Living Dictionaries*, online ed., "mindfulness."

value—and the habits that define that value—requires mindfulness as an unspoken foundational habit. At a second glance, we can even see how Alcoa's worker safety value and its defining habits also demand mindfulness. Recall the unit president's action plan at Alcoa. It relies on worker safety suggestions to create a plan ensuring that the same injury never happens again. This habit encourages workers to ask questions like, "Do I feel safe right now?" and "Do my colleagues feel safe right now?" and "Even if we *feel* safe, how could we *be* safer?" This sort of conscious examination of a present moment is another example of mindfulness.

Michael Acton Smith, the founder of Calm, gathers his team together every morning at 10 a.m. for a 10-minute daily meditation. He told *The Guardian* that if other workplaces adopted this ritual, "It would revolutionize workplaces around the world. And I know it sounds very Californian to meditate with your team, but it's wonderful. Everyone loves it. It's a very important tradition here. That's because in any high-stress job, you do get yanked around a lot by emotions, and meditation helps give you a little more perspective. It helps you ride the waves of life better."[191] Value-driven habits demand mindfulness. For some organizations, mindfulness is an explicit habit in its own right; for others, mindfulness is a (perhaps unspoken) foundational habit for other value-driven habits.

Unconventional Habits: Mindfulness, Meditation, and the Marines

When you think of the Marine Corps, you probably think of a group of tough, no-nonsense, "Oorah!" people who fiercely go into battle: a band of brothers and sisters fighting machine. You don't think of a group of people who sit around and meditate. It's not what warriors do. Well, you'd be wrong.

---

[191] Ian Tucker, "Michael Acton Smith: 'We want to show meditation is common sense,'" *The Guardian*, October 8, 2017, https://www.theguardian.com/technology/2017/oct/08/michael-acton-smith-meditation-common-sense-moshi-monsters-calm-app.

The U.S. military has been actively exploring the benefits of meditation and mindfulness. At first, not surprisingly, there was resistance. The Marines involved in an early experiment felt weird about it, until they saw results. As Major Jeffrey Davis, whose unit was trained in meditation before its 2008 Iraq deployment, told *Pacific Standard* magazine, "We look at all of these weapons systems around us as necessary for war. But it's the human mind that operates all these things. If I can find a better way to train a Marine—if I can teach him to react quicker, to think quicker, to learn quicker, to act wiser in an ambiguous situation—the better off we are."[192]

In an eight-week course called "Mindfulness-Based Mind Fitness Training," led by Elizabeth A. Stanley, a former Army intelligence officer and Georgetown University security-studies professor, the Marines learned techniques meant to focus attention, release wandering thoughts, and use awareness to help the body and mind self-regulate during and after stressful experiences. Amishi Jha, a cognitive neuroscientist at the University of Miami, tested the Marines before and after the course. The result was that those who practiced mindfulness reported an improved ability to handle stress and both retain and regain focus. Since then much larger groups of Marines have gone through mindfulness programs as the Pentagon considers implementation on a much grander scale.[193]

In another study, the brains of eight platoons of Marines were scanned using fMRI (which detects blood flow) before going through combat scenarios. Four of the eight platoons also went through an eight-week mindfulness course. All eight platoons went through combat scenarios at the Infantry Immersion Trainer. The Marines trained in mindfulness technique displayed a better recovery from stressful training, and their brain scans had similar neural patterns to those of elite performers—the

---

[192] Brian Mockenhaupt, "A State of Military Mind," *Pacific Standard*, June 18, 2012, https://psmag.com/social-justice/a-state-military-mind-42839.
[193] Ibid.

SEALs and Olympians.[194]

For the Marines, mindfulness didn't form the foundation for another habit. Mindfulness *was* the habit. By practicing mindfulness, Marines could think faster, handle stress better, and recover quicker. In short: they performed better.[195]

Mindfulness That Produces:
Yoga at Aetna

In stark contrast, let's move from the marines to insurance agents. Aetna, the $60 billion insurance giant, tested a mindfulness program along with "gentle yoga" with hundreds of thousands of its workers. At the end of 10 weeks, self-reported stress levels were reduced and, of even greater interest, biometric measurements (e.g., heart rate and cortisol) were reduced, showing that the effects weren't merely psychosomatic. In other words, it wasn't just in their minds: there was physical proof, too. In addition, participants reported a better night's sleep, reduced pain, and higher productivity.[196]

End result: just from this single program, Aetna says it saved about $2,000 per employee in healthcare costs and gained about $3,000 per employee in productivity.[197] Mindfulness has its rewards!

New York Times business reporter, David Gelles, revealed the Aetna story in his book *Mindful Work*, along with examples from other companies, such as General Mills, Green Mountain Coffee, Google, Ford, and LinkedIn, all who have seen the wisdom of implementing mindfulness programs. Wondering about top business executives who have advocated for mindfulness? Try Steve Jobs, Jeff Weiner, Bill Ford, Larry Brilliant, Oprah Winfrey, and Ray Dalio.

---

[194] Ibid.

[195] Ibid.

[196] Joe Pinsker, "Corporations' Newest Hack: Meditation," *The Atlantic*, March 10, 2015, https://www.theatlantic.com/business/archive/2015/03/corporations-newest-productivity-hack-meditation/387286/.

[197] Ibid.

"Meditation more than anything in my life was the biggest ingredient of whatever success I've had," said Ray Dalio.[198] His success? He just happens to be the billionaire founder of Bridgewater Associates, one of the world's largest hedge fund firms, managing $150 billion in assets.

Meditation at Google

Even high tech has logged on to mindfulness and meditation. In fact, at Google, there's often a six-month waiting list to attend a class called "Search Inside Yourself" created by veteran engineer Chade-Meng Tan.[199]

By branding meditation as an emotional intelligence workout, Meng (as he's informally known) positioned his class as a contemplative training program to help people better relate to themselves and others—a skill-set many people might feel was lacking in the nerdy, engineer-heavy Silicon Valley culture.

"I'm not interested in bringing Buddhism to Google," Meng has said. "I am interested in helping people at Google find the key to happiness."[200] Meng thinks big. His job description reads: "Enlighten minds, open hearts, create world peace." *Business Reporter* magazine reported that Search Inside Yourself has three key elements :

- **Attention training:** No matter what happens when you're under duress, you have the skill to bring the mind to a place that's calm and clear.

- **Self-knowledge:** Once your mind is calm and clear, you can create a quality of self-awareness that evolves into self-mastery and control your emotions.

- **Creating mental habits:** Take, for example, the mental habit of

---

[198] James Saft, "Meditation and the art of investment," *Reuters*, April 17, 2013, http://blogs.reuters.com/james-saft/2013/04/17/meditation-and-the-art-of-investment/.
[199] Drake Baer, "Here's What Google Teaches Employees In Its 'Search Inside Yourself' Course," *Business Insider*, August 5, 2014, http://www.businessinsider.com/search-inside-yourself-googles-life-changing-mindfulness-course-2014-8.
[200] Ibid.

kindness and wanting everyone to be happy. Says Meng, "Once that becomes a habit, you don't have to think about it; it just comes naturally."[201]

According to a Google spokesperson, the class is effective because of the way it ties neuroscience to the first-person research that mediators have been doing for some 2,500 years.[202] As with the Marines and Aetna, Google encouraged its Tribe to adopt mindfulness and meditation as daily habits, and increased Tribe happiness followed.

What's It All Mean?

Summing it up, we're saying that mindfulness is the most foundational habit of all, in that it is required to break old habits and form new ones. Take changing one's diet for instance. The habit of eating poorly isn't one that can be fixed without making conscious decisions about setting down the hamburger and picking up the salad fork. It takes conscious moments like that all day long to change a bad habit into a good one. And to adopt a new habit requires conscious choices made through daily mindfulness.

Habits help us live out our values. That's an essential premise. In a way, we are proposing two frameworks. One: a broad framework that must be tailored to each organization (habits, values, purpose). Two: a prescribed framework with mindfulness (the most foundational habit) as the core habit that leads to Tribe happiness, which leads to increased productivity toward some business objective (mindfulness, Tribe happiness, productivity).

We recommend that organizations should acknowledge the role of mindfulness as a foundational habit for the other value-driven habits they create as they flush out their purposes, values, and habits. Whether your organization is looking to make your values actionable or to utilize personal growth to create impact on business objectives, there is an undeniable connection between "doing" and "being." Habits play a key

---

[201] Ibid.
[202] Ibid.

role in making an intention become a reality.

2020: Professional Habits

We make no excuse for wheeling out our favorite Ancient Greek philosopher one more time. Aristotle, pupil of Plato and teacher of Alexander the Great, said a few wise things in his time (384–322 BCE). Among them is, "Excellence is an art won by training and habituation. We do not act rightly because we have virtue or excellence, but we rather have those because we have acted rightly. We are what we repeatedly do. Excellence, then, is not an act but a habit."

Yes, he's our favorite philosopher and this is our favorite quote. We all want to strive for excellence, and what was good enough for Aristotle 2,400 years ago is good enough for us today. Good habits are the key. How to acquire them is the next step in our journey together.

Of course, establishing positive habits is also all about personal growth, a new dimension greatly underestimated by many organizations. Personal growth stems from a conscious decision and effort to take control of your life. It's not easy. Change is always difficult. And there are plenty of barriers. One such barrier is that most of us have little awareness of how we spend our time and what motivates us to do so. Research suggests that 40 percent of daily activity is habitual and not planned.[203] We don't consciously program our day's undertakings. So, who is really in control here, and where did these habitual behaviors come from?

Step one toward changing our behavior is to raise our awareness about the things we do automatically that get in the way of change. Step two is to create new automatic responses to replace the old; to come up with responses and thoughts that ease us ever closer to our goals and the ability to live our true personal values. Successful behavior change continues by taking small, easy steps. Achieving them keeps us motivated to progress to

---

[203] Valerie A. Curtis, Lisa O. Danquah, and Robert V. Aunger, "Planned, motivated and habitual hygiene behaviour: an eleven country review," *Health Education Research* 24, no. 4 (March 2009): 655-673.

more difficult challenges as we build momentum and self-efficacy. What this means is that even seemingly inconsequential changes to our routines can forge profound effects on our personal lives if they are regularly repeated. These micro-actions become habits that we perform without thinking about them. The barriers have been removed. It's the same with organizations as it is with people. Small behaviors repeated consistently and reliably by the Tribe determine an organization's culture and ultimate success.

The conclusion: because there is a strong link between personal development and organizational success, smart organizations take responsibility to promote the personal growth of their Tribe.

Company leaders, therefore, should deliver opportunities that empower every employee to overcome any obstacles to behavior change, and thereby flourish. The kinds of personal development goals that are beneficial for individuals are more or less the same as those that a thriving enterprise needs. Increasing focus, productivity, and mindfulness are good for the person, good for the organization, and good for the planet. We recognize it may be difficult to practice new habits without first practicing a new state of mind, so see Appendix A for a discussion on mindfulness and meditation. Personal growth leads to professional growth, which leads to organizational success. The link: the formation of Professional Habits.

ProHabits is the Glue

Our conclusion, from our countless hours of reading, discussing, and interviewing 500+ organizational leaders living these realities, is that professional habits serve a critical role in purpose transformation. This inspired us to find a life and career altering purpose: *elevate humanity in the workplace*. That's where ProHabits comes in, our new research platform for leaders and organizations to live their values. For Pamela Stroko, Vice President of HCM (Human Capital Management) Transformation and

Thought Leadership at Oracle, "ProHabits is like glue," and she's right.[204]

Good habits stick with you. They cement and solidify your culture. The delivery mechanism for this "glue" comes from our proprietary software, which delivers daily emails to you that focus on single habits that research has shown help your nurture and achieve your best self. That's our contemporary take on Maslow's concept of self-actualization.

As an example, data from our first cohort group indicates that focus, known as the "ProFocus Track," is among the most popular (read: productive) habit. One example activity asks the individual to write down on a card, "What is most important for you to focus on today?"; carry that card around, and appropriately align individual actions with this personally prioritized focus or goal.

Pamela observes that these daily feeds, "Help translate what we want to be to what we want to become, into the how we are going to do that and how we are going to live that every day. In order for something to be sustainable you have to get it into the culture…it's in the air…it's what we breathe. ProHabits is the vehicle to get you there."

She goes further. "ProHabits," she says, "gives you a sustainable engine to collectively and collaboratively work on individual career growth and organizational growth at the same time. In an age when companies can buy the same technology and develop similar strategies, your only sustainable advantage is your people. Organizations, therefore, need to offer a creative and passionate environment to empower your people and accomplish your goals as an organization." You can sign up for a free 30-day trial of this program at ProHabits.com.

Driving It Home

We began this book by discussing Simon Sinek's *Start with Why*. Reading this remarkable book and watching his sensational TED Talk

---

[204] Pamela Stroko (Vice President of HCM Transformation and Thought Leadership at Oracle) in discussion with the author.

inspired us to put together a plan for senior executives and others passionate about change and transformation to find and implement their Why within their organizations. That's the plan you've hopefully absorbed through these pages. Now, we want to go even further. In the same way that we wanted to turn Simon Sinek's "Why" into something actionable, we want to turn the concept of Professional Habits into something actionable.

If you have found value in this book, we invite you to participate in one of the world's largest research projects that is inspiring and monitoring progressing company cultures. We look forward to connecting with you directly. Please feel free to reach out at Mabbly.com and ProHabits.com.

Feed the wolf that matters!

Kind Regards, Adam & Hank

Acknowledgements

This book wouldn't exist without these inspired human beings, we appreciate all that you do:

Andy Swindler, Contributing Author

Gennadiy (Gena) Chigrinov, Contributor

Kayla M. Stevens, M.A.

Malcolm Nicholl

Lisa Provenzano

Chris L. Johnson, PsyD

Michael M. Shuster, Ph.D

Rachel Pollard

Alex Blair

Vlad Moldavskiy

LeeAna Theberg

Nicholas Kosirog-Jones

Brad Hettich

Jason Richmond

The Breakfast Club

Gratitude

Thank you to the companies who shared its story
and taught us along the way.

@properties

AAR Corp.

Algolia

ARCA

Baird & Warner

Baker Tilly

Beach House Group

Benchprep

Bernie's Book Bank

Blue Plate Catering

Brilliant

Brindley

Bucketfeet

Bunker Labs

BW Container Systems

Cars.com

CASE Construction Equipment

Chicago Bar Company, LLC/RXBAR

Clorox

Compass Group

Computer Aided Technology

Couchbase

CoverHound

Coyote Logistics

DePaul University's Coleman Entrepreneurship Center

DuPuis Group

Flexera

Freshii

Ganeden Inc

GE

Giles and Associates

Griffith Foods

Hill-Rom

Hillard Heintze

IIDA

Innovative Office Solutions

Iron Galaxies

ISACA

IT Savvy

Jellyvision

JetBlue

Label Insight

Levenfeld Pearlstein, LLC

Lincoln Park Zoo

Lyric Opera

Microsoft

Northwestern University

Omron

OR Movement

Oracle

Pantheon Enterprises

Patagonia Inc.

Payline Data

Perma-Seal Basement Systems

Power Home Remodeling

Provident Trust

Shure Incorporated

Simon Sinek

SnackNation

Sunset Foods

Threshold

tilr

Tovar Snow

TRN Staffing

Tuthill Corporation

UL

Wilson Sporting Goods/ Louisville Slugger

Yoobi

Zappos Insights

Appendix A: When You Think It's Too Much to Change – Major Workplace Transformations in History

1922: The 40-Hour Week

The Ford Motor Company was one of the pioneers of a five-day, 40-hour week. Explaining the decision to reduce workdays to five a week, company president Edsel Ford said, "Every man needs more than one day a week for rest and recreation...The Ford Motor Company has always sought to promote [an] ideal home life for its employees. We believe that in order to live properly every man should have more time to spend with his family."[205]

Company founder Henry Ford, Edsel's father, commented, "It is high time to rid ourselves of the notion that leisure for workmen is either 'lost time' or a class privilege." These are noble thoughts from a man whose aim was to, "Put the world on wheels" by producing an affordable vehicle for the general public. This was not even Ford's first pioneering business practice. In 1914, the Ford Motor Company nearly doubled the minimum wage of its male workers to $5 per eight-hour day.[206] While it shocked the rest of the industry, it was a stroke of genius, as it boosted productivity and pride among the workers. The 40-hour week was a move in the same mold.

1987: Smoking Gets Banned

Once upon a time, people smoked anywhere and everywhere. But in 1987, Boeing, the giant Seattle-based airplane manufacturer, was one of

---

[205] "Ford Factory Workers Get 40-hour Week," History, May 1, 2017, accessed November 28, 2017, http://www.history.com/this-day-in-history/ford-factory-workers-get-40-hour-week.
[206] Ibid

the first major companies to institute a ban on smoking in all company offices, although, it was still allowed on the factory floor.[207] Nevertheless, it was a big step. "I would expect [the] reaction to this latest ban to be overwhelmingly positive," said company spokesman Lee Lathrop. No surprise there, as 72 percent of the company's 115,000 workers at the time were non-smokers. But 30 years ago, Boeing was in the vanguard of the anti-cigarette movement designed to make workplaces healthier.[208]

2010: Wellness Accelerates

"'Wellness,' there's a word you don't hear every day." That's what CBS's Dan Rather intoned when he presented a *60 Minutes* segment on wellness in 1979. But the *New York Times* referencing the TV segment in its own coverage of wellness in 2010 commented, "… [M]ore than three decades later 'wellness' is, in fact, a word that Americans might hear every day."[209]

How times change. The *Global Wellness Institute* went on to highlight the remarkable impact that the concept of wellness has had across the globe, reaching a dramatic tipping point where, "A concept of wellness transforms every industry from food and beverage to travel."[210]

Health-conscious companies not only focus on the needs of their clients and consumers, but also on the needs of members of their Tribe, knowing that for younger generations it is a major consideration in joining or remaining with a company. Far-sighted corporations today offer on-site health and wellness centers. They entice and reward workers with everything from juice bars to quiet zones for meditation, from special pods where you can take a nap, to state-of-the-art gyms where you can work up

[207] "The Boeing Co. Announced Friday It Will Ban Smoking…," *UPI*, February 27, 1987, https://www.upi.com/Archives/1987/02/27/The-Boeing-Co-announced-Friday-it-will-ban-smoking/4699541400400/.
[208] Ibid.
[209] Ben Zimmer, "Wellness," *The New York Times*, April 17, 2010, http://www.nytimes.com/2010/04/18/magazine/18FOB-onlanguage-t.html.
[210] "The History of Wellness," *Global Wellness Institute*, https://www.globalwellnessinstitute.org/history-of-wellness/.

a sweat between conference calls. Healthy and happy workers equal proud and productive workers.

2014: $3.4-Trillion Market

We've talked about the accelerating pace of change, so consider this: in 2014 The Global Wellness Institute unveiled research showing that the worldwide wellness industry represented a $3.4-trillion market.[211] That's incredibly significant when you realize it's 3.4 times larger than the global pharmaceutical industry.

What's next? The only constant is change and more change. Throughout the book, we have discussed the value of Tribe members who make a contribution and are recognized for their contribution. Individuals benefit, organizations benefit, and the world at large benefits.

Some excellent research substantiates the value of discovering one's roadmap to a best self which, as part of the journey, abandons the old concept of a division between our work self and our personal life. Positive psychology, the study of human thriving, brings us closer. For further study, we recommend three important books:

The Power of Habit: Why We Do What We Do in Life and Business by Pulitzer Prize-winning business reporter Charles Duhigg. It took the world by storm when it was published in 2012 and went on to spend more than 60 weeks on the *New York Times* bestseller list. More than 4,000 Amazon reviews later, it boasts a 4½ star rating. At its core, *The Power of Habit* argues that understanding how habits work is the key to becoming more productive, building revolutionary companies and social movements, and achieving life and corporate success. It's an argument with which we obviously agree. Data gained from our ProHabits community echoes these findings.

---

[211] Beth McGroarty, "Global Wellness Institute Study: $3.4 Trillion Global Wellness Market is Now Three Times Larger Than Worldwide Pharmaceutical Industry," *Global Wellness Institute*, 2014, https://www.globalwellnessinstitute.org/global-wellness-institute-study-34-trillion-global-wellness-market-is-now-three-times-larger-than-worldwide-pharmaceutical-industry.

The Happiness Advantage: The Seven Principles of Positive Psychology That Fuel Success and Performance at Work by Shawn Achor. A former Harvard researcher, Achor turns on its head the premise that, "Success leads to happiness."[212] Rather, he says, it is the opposite: "Happiness leads to success." Achor draws on his own research—including one of the largest studies of happiness and potential—and uses stories and case studies from his work with thousands of *Fortune 500* executives in 42 countries to explain how we can reprogram our brains to become more positive in order to gain a competitive edge at work.

Tools of Titans: The Tactics, Routines, and Habits of Billionaires, Icons, and World-Class Performers by Timothy Ferriss. Ferriss, well-known for his previous best-seller, *The 4-Hour Workweek,* interviewed more than 200 world-class performers ranging from superstar celebrities to athletes, and from legendary Special Operations commanders to black-market biochemists, to distil their tactics, routines, and habits.[213]

---

[212] "The Happiness Advantage," Shawn Achor, http://www.shawnachor.com/the-books/the-happiness-advantage/.
[213] "Intro," Tools of Titans, https://toolsoftitans.com/intro/#main.

Appendix B: They Live It

Who better to guide your purpose transformation than the companies who have gone before you? Read on for inspiring stories of companies who put people over profits and realized both tangible and intangible benefits in return.

***

Company: Tuthill Corporation

Location: Burr Ridge, Illinois

Business/Organization: Manufacturer of pumps, meters, vacuum systems, and blowers

Purpose: Wake the World

Imagine a company so concerned about its employees' health that it purchased the patent for a steam-powered truck just so it could ease their workload. "Steam-powered" is probably your first clue that it didn't just happen yesterday. In fact, it happened over a hundred years ago. And, quite remarkably, the beneficiaries were the company's employees with four legs, not two.

Tuthill Corporation, one of today's leading manufacturers of industrial pumps, brought in those steam-powered trucks to save the hearts of horses that hauled heavy loads of clay from the quarry. Back then, Tuthill, "Made the bricks that helped make Chicago."

From the beginning, when James B. Tuthill founded the business in 1892, Tuthill was a company with heart. It's a company that recognizes being a purpose-driven organization is a continuing journey—an ever-changing journey—and that, therefore, the ultimate destination may never be reached. It's one of the companies that epitomize the five stages we've identified: Believe, Discover, Ignite, Express, and Impact.

Believe

Tuthill is happy to talk about what it sells; it's even happier to talk about what it believes. It's remained a family-owned business with family values. Current (and fourth-generation) owner Jay Tuthill, remembers his father as a stern, stoic businessman with a huge heart and a soft spot for human dignity. He was concerned about everything—even the bathrooms.

In 2005, Jay decided to take that concern even further and extend the legacy beyond one lifetime and beyond the company. Chad Gabriel, the company's Director of Seismic Branding, says, "It took quite a leap of faith to invest in discovering our purpose, but Tuthill did it and we haven't looked back since."

One of its first steps was to become a dedicated conscious company, so the Tuthill leadership developed a three-pronged vision: 1) build an ingenious company, 2) support flourishing families, and 3) impact spirited communities.

The third prong—some might say a grandiose goal—was the challenge. When Chad became responsible for the Tuthill brand in 2011, he was charged with finding a better, simpler way to express their purpose. What was their "Why?"

Discover

The three prongs were fundamental to the core culture of the company. But the company felt there had to be a more succinct way to sum up its belief.

What was its North Star? What was its goal, its destination that might never be reached? What would stretch it beyond its horizons? What was its "compass" that would guide the company on its journey?

It found its answer—something that is simple, genuine, and aspirational, something that shows an authentic desire to enhance the lives of people within their sphere of influence. The company discovered its Why: *Wake the world.* The Why was already there, Tuthill just had to find it. From the earliest days of the company and the desire to help the hearts of the horses, it had a history of being a conscious company. Now it had a future.

Ignite

But how would they get the Tuthill Tribe to care about and share the Why? How would they ignite passion for the long haul? Tuthill leadership knew it needed to wake its own people—to bring them truly alive—before it could wake the world. It wasn't easy. Getting people to unshackle from entrenched positions is never easy. Everyone was undoubtedly willing to work on making company pumps, but some weren't as willing to work on their own pumps—their hearts.

Tuthill's conscious leadership retreats were one means to this end. Company owner Jay Tuthill set an example by being one of the teachers and changing his title from Chief Executive Officer to Chief Environmental Officer, firmly displaying his dedication to create a wonderful place to work. Or, as Chad Gabriel puts it, to "Create the space for the heart to thrive." The retreats, he says, were occasions for participants to, "Unleash their inner aliveness."

It was an alien concept to many. In fact, at the first retreat someone asked, "So when are we going to get to the work training?" At that point it hit Chad that, "This is far from work training—this is life training."

It wasn't for everyone. Some weren't ready for change and left for more traditionally minded companies; others refocused their lives on family. This was fine with Tuthill, as the company Tribe became solidified into those who were truly committed.

Express

The Tuthill philosophy: "One by one we become many and a workforce becomes a life force." As CEO Tom Carmazzi says, "We have embarked on a journey that we believe will have impact outside of Tuthill, reaffirming, in fact, our purpose is to Wake the World." But how to do that beyond their own four walls? Tuthill took the plunge to expand their belief into, "A life full of curiosity, clarity, grit, grace, gratitude and love." According to Tuthill, "The creation of a conscious company that will wake the world does not happen by accident. In fact, it takes a lot. Even some math." Their formula: Awareness + Choice + Responsibility = Aliveness.

One of their first missions, in consultation with all stakeholders—including customers, employees, and board members—was to find an organization they could support. Their choice: Team Rubicon, a veteran-based disaster response volunteer organization, a mission that literally stands for aliveness.

You can tell what a perfect partner Team Rubicon is when you read its own purpose: "Through continued service, Team Rubicon seeks to provide our veterans with three things they lose after leaving the military: a purpose, gained through disaster relief; community, built by serving with others; and self-worth, from recognizing the impact one individual can make."[214]

Another way Tuthill Corporation expresses and shares its purpose is through its purpose portal WakeTheWorld.com. On the site, the company explains conscious culture and shares a set of tools to promote dialogue and highlight how everyone can be a conscious leader in life.

Impact

What kind of impact is Tuthill making? How does the company measure it? Tuthill closely monitors the number of employees engaged, the dollars raised and dollars donated, and the number of events it organizes or in which it participates. In 2016 some 35 percent of its Tribe have taken part in Team Rubicon and this number is on the rise.

---

[214] "Our Mission," Team Rubicon, https://teamrubiconusa.org/mission/.

"We know we'll be an ingenious company that supports flourishing families and spirited communities," says Chad Gabriel. "Being a conscious company is a journey—a journey committed to aliveness. Tuthill employees are invited to live into their personal greatness and lend a helping hand to others so that they too can be great."

The really amazing thing about Tuthill is that it doesn't limit its engagement to employees. The company's far-sighted altruism shows how a humanitarian focus can bring higher purpose to lives—and increased profits for their company.

As we've discussed, the discovery of purpose is a never-ending journey—something the Tuthill leadership fully comprehends and embraces. Chad acknowledges, "At times it can seem overwhelming, but knowing we have support from one another, we continue to climb. We may never reach our aspirational goal in our lifetimes, but we are laying the foundation for future generations." Far-sighted, indeed. No one ever said it was going to be easy.

During Tuthill's leadership's discovery of their purpose, they asked themselves: If Tuthill were gone tomorrow, what would the world miss about it? Another manufacturer could step in and make the pumps. But would those pumps fuel the heart like Tuthill does? Would that company be conscious of its impact on the wider world and actively seek to make the lives of its employees and the lives of people outside the company better? Would that company care about making its employees come alive as much as it cares about making money?

Probably not, because Tuthill is on a journey of its own and each company must make its own way down its own path. Tuthill's path is aptly summed up in this statement: "We believe that a company can be more than just an entity for making money, it can be a catalyst for change: a change in ourselves, others, and the world. We want to help people discover aliveness by creating space for hearts to thrive. Whether it's at home, at work, or in the community, we want people to realize they can have an astounding impact."[215]

Tuthill is impacting the world, one awakening at a time.

***

[215] Chad Gabriel (Director of Seismic Branding at Tuthill Corporation), in discussion with the author, May 2016

Company: Lyric Opera

Location: Chicago, Illinois

Business/Organization: Opera

Purpose: Igniting transformation through art

When you think about Opera, what comes to mind? Is it soaring music, riveting drama, and gorgeous costumes and sets? Perhaps you imagine yourself enjoying a captivating performance, or perhaps you're among the 99 percent of the world for whom opera has no relevance.

Either way, you can't help but be impressed by Chicago's prestigious Lyric Opera. It's a company that knows how to tell stories and how to express its mission—and with the highest caliber production values. Lyric Opera has an incredibly positive impact on the community through its stage productions and numerous educational programs. But the Opera company's story hasn't always been told effectively, especially to people for whom opera is an alien concept.

Lyric Opera's solution was a journey to discover their purpose. They knew they needed to become more relevant and were remarkably willing to recreate their own story from the inside out to accomplish that. As we listened to their stories, Adam suggested that, in reality, their purpose was *igniting transformation through art.* Immediately, the energy in the room changed. Everyone felt it: the surge of excitement. That's what happens when you identify your purpose—especially one that was there all along.

Lyric Opera was eager to keep the momentum going, so over the next few months, it concentrated on finding ways to become part of people's lives and for people to take part in the life of Lyric Opera. Its goal was to inspire people to use their own voices. Perhaps it's not surprising that one of the first things an opera company would think to do was getting people to sing. If you ask a group of kindergartners who can sing, they all raise their hands. With adults, not so much.

So, during a performance at Chicago's Millennium Park, Lyric Opera asked its audience to participate in a sing-along. How many opera companies ever do that? Imagine having the chance to sing with some of the best voices in the world? That would get you talking. And what better way to share that experience than through social media, which was fully embraced by both parties.

Perhaps, though, Lyric Opera's boldest idea was to create "Chicago Voices" as a way for people to tell their own stories of community. Here's what happened. Lyric Opera offered to provide professional guidance and experience so three groups could shape, stage, and ultimately perform their productions at the 1,500-seat Harris Theater. After identifying 11 finalists who wanted to tell their story, the final three, whose performances ranged from traditional music to navigating life with disabilities to a production about seniors, were selected by the public. Chicagoans enthusiastically supported the idea. More than 13,000 cast votes to select the final three, and the performance quickly sold out.

Lyric Opera has accomplished so much and it has plans for much more, starting with igniting its purpose within its core team of 111 people. In addition to using its purpose to find innovative ways to become relevant to people's lives, Lyric Opera also plans to change existing activities so even more voices can be heard. And through it all, Lyric Opera will continue to hold its "Why" as its guiding light. As Senior Director of Communications Holly Gilson told us, "Everything we do gets measured against the Why."

Holly frankly admits there have been some struggles getting everyone on board to sing the same tune. Remember, no one said it was going to be easy. "We're not quite there yet," she says, "But it's coming together, and following our Why gives everyone a reason to unite under our director's leadership. We work together well, but this will allow us to work better. 'Igniting transformation through art' are four words everyone knows and this is the direction in which we're sailing."[216]

Lyric Opera's General Director, President, and CEO Anthony Freud, puts it this way: "Finding a sense of common purpose, finding a sense of shared ambition, finding a regular means of communicating in a way that achieves the right results across the company is a wonderfully complex management task, indeed challenge, within an opera company."

Anthony feels that we're living in a complicated, confusing, and disturbing world with more people concerned about the state of their lives than at any point in his lifetime, adding, "I think in that context, art has an ever more important powerful role to play in allowing people to develop a better understanding of some of the issues, problems, and challenges of all our lives and making them better able to engage with some of those challenges. We, as a great opera company, have to be conscious of that as a new and growing responsibility and have to ensure that everything we do understands the role that we play in allowing people to grapple in a more effective way with some of life's complications. And that of course brings us right back to our Why, which is igniting transformation through art."[217]

It's no surprise that an opera company has fine-tuned a way to Express its purpose to the world.

***

---

[216] Holly Gilson (Senior Director of Communications at Lyric Opera) in discussion with the author, May 2016.
[217] Anthony Freud (General Director, President, and CEO at Lyric Opera) in discussion with the author, May 2016.

Company: AAR Corp.

Location: Wood Dale, Illinois

Business/Organization: Global provider of aviation services

Purpose: Doing it right to better connect the world

When the leadership of AAR Corp. decided they needed to articulate a corporate purpose and refreshed values, they acted with the speed and efficiency that is the company's hallmark.

First, they brought an agency on board to help in the task, and then they consulted with stakeholders across their entire business spectrum. But once the top business leaders themselves sat in a room to finally define the purpose and values, it took no more than two hours. Agreement happened so fast that initially that they brought in a few employees working nearby for a credibility sniff test to make sure they were not off base, as Kathleen Cantillon, Vice President of Strategic Communications, told us.

The new purpose: *doing it right to connect a better world.* It's a perfect summation of what AAR Corp. is all about. The aviation aftermarket services firm knows it has to get it right because it's responsible for the maintenance and safety of commercial and military aircraft across the globe. There's zero margin for error. A mistake could prove fatal. And of course, the company and its team of more than 5,000 play a critical role in helping major airlines connecting people and businesses country to country.

While AAR Corp. can deliver some parts anywhere in the world within three hours—a time margin that's critical for cost-effective airline operations—the future is about more than parts and maintenance. It's about people.

AAR Corp.'s road to articulating its purpose began when CEO David P. Storch succeeded his father-in-law, company founder Ira A. Eichner, as Chairman of the Board. At the time, the company was still using a mission statement and principles that were established in the late 1990s. When the company strategically re-positioned in 2015, AAR Corp. believed that to continue to grow globally and have a positive impact on the rapidly changing aviation industry, it needed stronger brand awareness of its capabilities within the B2B supply chain.

Its new goal was to become best in class with a high-performance culture. Leaders believed that employees needed to be fully engaged in their workplace by aspiring to the company's higher purpose and living its values. And it was up to leadership to ignite this culture by clearly communicating its purpose and living its values.

Listen to how the company puts "Doing it right" into a larger context: "Right is not always easy. Right is not always patient. Right can be brave, demanding, and even unique. So, it was when women won the right to vote, when FedEx introduced next-day delivery, or when Amazon reinvented the supply chain. Right is about setting a direction, believing in what you are doing, and doing it well."

"At AAR Corp., we constantly search for the right thing to do for our customers, for our employees, for partners, and for society. We wake up in the morning knowing we have to deliver, and at the end of the day, believe we did our best, and are encouraged to return the next day and do even better. We do not rest on our earlier accomplishments."

Kathleen, whose 30-year career focused primarily on external communications, admits that her first experience of igniting a company's culture was a bit daunting, but she definitely did it right. Here's how:

Step One: Created compelling collateral materials to simultaneously convey the new vision to all teams around the world, including:

1. A values video on YouTube developed in conjunction with the outside firm that featured employee peers and not just leadership.

2. A PowerPoint presentation that showcased the purpose framework and was distributed for local playback to avoid technology screen share issues.

3. A flipbook for each employee outlining purpose and values for quick and convenient desk reference.

4. Giveaways promoting the new purpose.

Key managers in each location were trained on the new purpose and materials, and charged with customizing them for local consumption.

Step Two: Coordinated with top managers a couple of weeks before the launch and conducted breakout sessions to discuss how the new purpose and values framework would be relevant to each manager's workforce and how to communicate it in a way that would resonate with each team. The managers were trained and inspired to lead local sessions on Purpose launch day that were broken into two parts:

1. A global live telephone broadcast from the CEO (which was also recorded for those who couldn't attend in person due to time difference, etc.).

2. An on-site airing of the purpose/values video followed by an open forum for employees and their managers to discuss what this meant for them and their area of business.

Step Three: Kept momentum going. For reinforcement, the AAR Corp. employee media hub was updated with sections devoted to "Doing it right." An online course was pushed to all employees. Each week, a story highlighting an office or employee living a value was shared through their intranet. Local managers also developed recognition tokens, which they gave to employees who were living the newfound Why, "Doing it right."

AAR Corp. even launched a #DoingItRight hashtag for use on social media. And performance appraisals began to include the new values as part of employee evaluation and goal setting. Additionally, knowing that the best ideas often come from the people doing the work, AAR Corp. provided financial incentives for ideas that generated revenue and saved costs. The new purpose and values have also found their way into hiring and training processes, since this is the best time to assess if someone is a good match for the company culture.

How did the workforce respond to the new purpose of, "Doing it right?" In a company-wide survey conducted a few months after launch, 63 percent said they felt inspired and 66 percent believed it would make AAR Corp. a better place to work: a high acceptance rate when you consider many workers' natural skepticism, especially longer-term employees.[218] How are they doing? They're doing it right!

***

---

[218] Kathleen Cantillon (Vice President of Strategic Communications at AAR Corp.) in discussion with the author, September 2016.

Company: Coyote Logistics

Location: Chicago, Illinois

Business/Organization: Transportation and Logistics

Purpose: Do the right thing every time

How does a company go from being a startup freight brokerage to one that's valued at more than $1.8 billion and has grown to more than 2,000 employees in under a decade? Chicago-based Coyote Logistics has the answer. Hire the right people, train them, and give them the tools they need to succeed. Build a motivated workforce by hiring people who tend to be motivated in the first place. In short, *do the right thing every time.*

Former Chief Marketing Officer Jodi Navta told us, "The right fit is so important. This business is one where you're always 'on.' You have to find people that can handle this kind of fast-paced environment; people who can hustle, who want to make a difference, and aren't afraid to fail or to lead."

"We look for people that fit our culture. We hire a lot of athletes, people who worked multiple jobs at a time through college, or who've held leadership positions in student organizations. We look for smart people that can handle pressure. Then we train them to do the right things, make good decisions, and give them a chance to contribute to the business in a real, tangible way."

Coyote Logistics ignites its purpose through an internal media hub it calls "The Den," which shares stories about members of its Tribe who are making a difference one way or another. Jodi told us that The Den was inspired by a series of events that she witnessed early on during her career at Coyote Logistics. She witnessed the incredible response of Coyote Logistics employees in 2011 when Hurricane Irene caused more than $125 billion of destruction and at least 56 deaths. Within 30 minutes of the company's CEO asking for people to volunteer to be on call during the weekend to help, 100+ employees stepped forward to help customers move water, generators, and other emergency goods. Many worked flat out for three days, taking sleep breaks on the office floor.

"It was incredibly impressive," says Jodi. "So, I went home and wrote a love letter about everything I saw that weekend—the communication, motivation, the leadership, and the genuine respect that our Coyotes had not only for each other, but for our customers and the carriers we work with every day. The love letter was sent out the Monday morning after that weekend and generated tons of responses from others around the company thanking me for sharing the stories from that weekend, and telling the story of how we get things done in a way that resonated through the entire organization. I got responses from a huge portion of our employee base in the form of more stories from over the years. People really wanted to recognize each other and each other's successes. Now I had more stories to share from every part of the organization."

That spirit of recognition has continued with The Den, which is very visual—lots of photos and videos—designed to appeal to and ignite Millennials who make up a large part of Coyote Logistic's workforce. The employees contribute many of the ideas for content. Internal communication also comes via a monthly newsletter and CEO letters.

It all forms part of what Coyote Logistics feels makes the company great—teamwork. Jodi said, "We pride ourselves on what we call the pack mentality. Everything is team-based. It's essential. That's why we prefer to hire people who've shown they thrive in and understand teamwork."

Of course, she says, teamwork starts at the top: "One of the things that we've found works well is the 'mom and pop' approach that our founders took when it came to building the company. We have a lot of people here who have deep personal relationships—some with long-standing friendships through employee referrals, and so there's a close linkage between our team's work and personal relationships." [219]

When you band together, culture can drive an organization forward in unimaginable ways!

***

---

[219] Jodi Navta (Former Chief Marketing Officer at Coyote Logistics) in discussion with the author, March 2016.

Company: Blue Plate Catering

Location: Chicago, Illinois

Business/Organization: Catering/Hospitality

Purpose: Happy people making people happy

When Blue Plate Catering came into being it was just Jim Horan, his van, a vision, and a quickly growing reputation for delivering delicious fare. Today, the company has 145 full-time employees and 313 part-timers; it is recognized as Chicago's premier, award-winning catering company; and it recently moved into a newly constructed, 80,000 square foot, state-of-the-art facility.

In 1983, when Jim left his career in social work, he began by catering small jobs in the film industry. He turned his passion into a business that continues to grow. How did he do it? From day one, he's been dedicated to making people happy, a mission that Blue Plate formalized in 2015 into its corporate purpose statement: *happy people making people happy.*

Jim told us, "That's at the core of what we do. We love creating shared experiences that enrich people's lives. Our enthusiasm for food and service, along with our thirst for knowledge and growth, drive us to deliver innovative and memorable hospitality. We show this in big and small ways every day with each other, our clients, and partners."

To establish his purpose, Jim set up a Mission Vision Values Action Team—an internal group of cross-departmental staff members. Once they'd nailed it down, the action team came up with a plan to "Ignite" throughout the company. It started by conducting departmental presentations in early 2016 to share it with staff members and incorporate it into annual company, departmental, and individual goals.

According to Jim, "In my previous career as a social worker, I was keenly aware of the many aspects of community life and the importance of integrity, collaboration, and communication, all in the pursuit of happiness.

I was helping people solve problems, albeit problems which were certainly quite different than the ones posed by catering clients looking for food services. At the core of all this is promoting the betterment of relationships with everyone we work with including co-workers, vendors, clients, and everyone we encounter throughout the day. We aim to be friendly, helpful and positive, always striving to exceed people's expectations. This type of behavior makes for an excellent foundation for achieving our goals."

Internally, Blue Plate Catering tracks successes and shares recognition through its shout-out program. Every week, the human resources department publishes the "Newsflash" newsletter that includes shout-outs from peers, supervisors, clients, and partners. "Thankfully, the shout-outs are plentiful. Each week, we read about a happy client at an event or the extra effort that a driver made when making a delivery," says Jim.

Blue Plate Catering also hosts an annual "All Hands Meeting" for full-time staff to review the prior year and share the outlook and goals for the year ahead. At the same event, they honor employees with 5, 10, 15, 20, and 25-year service awards. Ignition!

Jim adds, "Our 'why' has made a big difference in helping us focus on our work. We always come back to the idea that whatever the task at hand, it's about being happy so you can make others happy—whether you work in the accounting department or are on the front lines at a catered event. Each day, we endeavor to communicate this message through our actions. When employees, clients, vendors, and partners are happy, it means that all the right pieces are coming together at the right time."

Blue Plate Catering values and focuses on dynamic growth from within through Wild Blue, an entrepreneurial incubator program that's one initiative of another endeavor set up by Jim called Round the Table Hospitality (RTTH). The Wild Blue program is designed to give employees of RTTH the opportunity to present great business ideas that they are passionate about, but might not have the necessary resources or opportunity to pursue on their own. The goal of this program is to encourage employees to participate in defining the RTTH brand, while at the same time providing a consistent process to assist the senior leadership team in making well-informed, strategic decision as they consider new business opportunities.

According to Jim, "We've grown the company from the inside out, focusing on a collaborative corporate culture, delivering exceptional customer service, building strong community relationships, and supporting those who have contributed to the organization's success. We truly believe that we are 'Happy people making people happy.'"[220]

Blue Plate Catering is serving up a hearty helping of purpose and that's the recipe for a happy culture.

***

---

[220] Jim Horan (CEO at Blue Plate Catering) in discussion with the author, February 2017.

Company: Freshii

Location: Toronto, Canada

Business/Organization: Quick service restaurant: healthy, fast, and casual

Purpose: Helping citizens of the world live better by making healthy food convenient and affordable

When 23-year-old Matthew Corrin was living in New York City, he frequented one-off fresh food "mom and pop" delis, but he noticed that they had little branding and offered a lackluster experience. It inspired him to think on a grander scale. Why not build a brand with the mission and purpose of making healthy fresh food affordable and convenient to all demographics around the world? Why not add some magic to the fast food business? Why not eliminate the excuse that people don't eat well because they cannot access healthy food, often blaming the high price tag and limited availability?

With no restaurant experience and no hard business plan, but driven by the power of his own vision and conviction, in 2005 Matthew opened his first Freshii location in Toronto. Today, Freshii is one of the fastest-growing restaurant brands in the world with more than 300 franchise locations in 15 countries.

Freshii's Chief People Officer, Ashley Dalziel, told us, "While the company has grown significantly, our purpose continues to drive everything we do—from our menu to our pricing to our store design. We feel we are energizing the world, one Freshii restaurant at a time."

A fast-casual restaurant with a unique and powerful concept, Freshii offers delicious and diverse options designed to energize people on-the-go. The company's in-house nutritionist creates every bowl, salad, wrap, snack, soup, smoothie, and juice, and the menu is constantly evolving as they incorporate the latest health food trends from around the world, all without sacrificing taste or price. Freshii offers superfoods like kale, quinoa, and turmeric, as well as brown rice, black beans, lean proteins, and healthy fats. Every item is customizable and therefore able to accommodate any dietary preference, making Freshii a restaurant that truly has no "veto vote"—there is something for everyone. Ashley says, "We like to think of it as a 'fast-fashion' retail model, similar to Zara. We take health trends from around the world, and bring them to the masses. Our goal is to make health and wellness accessible to everybody, everywhere."

Once the corporate purpose was established, *(helping citizens of the world live better by making healthy food convenient and affordable)*, Matthew Corrin developed five guiding principles to shape how the company operated:

1. Talk is cheap. Execution sets you apart.

2. Launch fast, fail fast, iterate faster.

3. Numbers rule.

4. Build a company with a killer culture, not a culture that kills your company.

5. Pick your battles.

Over a decade later, these principles are still followed every day, by every member of the Freshii Tribe, both at the corporate level and franchise partner level. In fact, they are prominently displayed on the wall at Freshii HQ as a daily reminder of the beliefs on which the company was founded.

Ashley told us, "We don't see ourselves as just a restaurant brand, limited to the four walls of the store. We will continue to innovate so that we can offer guests healthy meals in a way that is convenient and affordable—and the way this looks might change over time. Energizing the world is who we are and why we exist. Now, our focus is on executing that mission. We're constantly learning, improving and iterating in all aspects of our business. Our goal today is to open 800 stores by the end of 2019, but that's not all. Expect to see other innovations from us that impact how people access healthy food around the globe." That's a big goal—but Freshii only thinks big.

Take this comment from Ashley, for instance: "Freshii will redefine what a restaurant is and completely alter people's eating habits. Bowls and salads will be chosen over burgers and fries. Life expectancy will go up. Sickness and obesity will decrease. We'll create a healthier world where every demographic has access to high quality, fresh food without worry. It may sound lofty, but that's our Why. Freshii will change the way the world eats. Every single person who works at Freshii feels that this is so much more than 'just a job.'"

Naturally, without any prompting, the hashtag of #iiforever emerged, which was reflecting a sentiment of the workforce that they expect to be part of this purpose-driven company over the long term. This is quite exceptional for a largely Millennial team, a demographic that is typically thought of as being flighty and not loyal to an employer, says Ashley.

In early 2017, Freshii launched its internal global media hub called Communitii, designed so franchise partners could find resources, ask questions, read the latest Freshii news, and share ideas amongst themselves or directly with the Freshii HQ team. Adds Ashley, "It allows us to keep a pulse on innovative ideas, connect "Freshii People" around the globe on shared goals, and also foster a sense of healthy competition through contests and rewards. With Communitii, we can create, empower, and celebrate Freshii champions across our global network."

How does this focus on purpose translate into business results? Freshii intends to triple its store count by 2019, while improving same store sales growth, and innovate business channels outside of the stores through things such as Meal Box and mobile platforms.

Ashley's final word: "It's crucial that we listen to our global Communitii of Freshii guests, team members, and owners so that we can iterate and evolve ahead of the curve and continue to offer the latest versions of health in the most convenient ways. We will continue to execute on our mission and help citizens live energized lives by offering healthy food in a convenient and affordable way. That North Star will never change."[221]

With Freshii guiding the way, there's hope for a healthier world.

***

---

[221] Ashley Dalziel (Chief People Officer at Freshii) in discussion with the author, March 2017.

Company: Patagonia Inc.

Location: Ventura, California

Business/Organization: High-quality outdoor clothing brand

Purpose: Use business to inspire and implement solutions to the environmental crisis

Environmental responsibility was an important value at Patagonia long before it became a buzzword. The maker of high-quality, ethically produced outdoor clothing has donated one percent of its sales to grassroots environmental organizations every year for more than 30 years.

It's part of founder Yvon Chouinard's decision to operate like a company that means to be in business for 100 years and beyond—a company that doesn't simply seek short-term profits, a company that intends to make an Impact on the planet.

Vincent Stanley, Patagonia's Director of Philosophy, says,"If you take that seriously, you tend to act a lot more responsibly toward your employees, customers, communities, and nature. Social and ecological good rarely align with quarterly financial goals, but they dovetail nicely over the medium and long term."[222]

Chouinard, himself, launching Tin Shed Ventures, an internal fund to help like-minded, responsible startups bring positive benefit to the environment, clearly laid out the need for a changing business climate. He wrote, "Economic growth for the past two centuries has been tied to an ever-spiraling carbon bonfire. Business-and human-success in the next 100 years must come from working with nature rather than using it up. That is a necessity, not a luxury as it's seen now in most business quarters."[223]

Patagonia's focus on quality, ethically produced products, and

---

[222] Vincent Stanley (Director of Philosophy at Patagonia) in discussion with the author, November 2016.
[223] "PATAGONIA Launches '$20 Million & Change,'" *Mountain Blog Europe*, May 29, 2013, http://www.mountainblog.eu/patagonia-launches-20-million-change/.

environmental responsibility is reflected in four words: reduce, repair, reuse, and recycle. Patagonia retail employees are trained to help customers choose their purchases thoughtfully. The company willingly repairs items for customers to prevent the need for replacement and also accepts every product the company makes back for recycling or repurposing.

Practices like these have impact. They attract customers who share the same values and are willing to pay higher prices associated with living those values—customers who abhor the lowest-priced, unsustainable, sweatshop-manufactured goods. They also attract like-minded employees.

Dean Carter, Vice President for Human Resources and Shared Services, says, "We're recognized internationally for our commitment to authentic product quality and environmental activism, having donated $82 million in support of grassroots environmental organizations since 1985."

"Our internal culture mirrors this mentality in every way. We hire employees who treat work as play and regard themselves as ultimate customers for the products they produce—people who love to spend as much time as possible in the mountains or the wild. The Patagonia culture rewards the team player."

While Patagonia has always valued non-traditional skills and experiences, it didn't always undertake the same philosophy in employee performance measurement. Dean admits, "For many years, Patagonia suffered from a traditional, hierarchical, and arduous performance management and goal-setting. We wanted a system that was more progressive in nature and which helped employees continue their growth throughout the year. We wanted our new process to reflect our values: transparency, collaboration, and improvement."

Successfully making this transition took on board employee engagement software from a company called HighGround. The program leverages objectives and key results (OKRs) to help employees set goals. It promotes a growth mindset by treating development as a regenerative process and taps into the power of the crowd.

Patagonia soon noticed an increase in the amount of conversations employees had with managers about their performance, and transparency was significantly enhanced through making 98 percent of personal goals visible to the organization. On top of that, employees who had asked for feedback and completed a check-in were more likely to have received higher bonuses, yet another benefit of the focus on dialogue and development.

For Patagonia, leading the fight to save the beautiful planet we call Mother Earth has made the voyage to prosperity that much more meaningful. It's easy to understand why Patagonia is the model for other companies that care about making a positive impact on the environment. How inspiring is a purpose that impacts not only people, but all living things?

***

Company: Bernie's Book Bank

Location: Lake Bluff, Illinois

Business/Organization: Non-profit book provider

Purpose: Books for a better life

The death of a parent often leads to some soul-searching on the part of the surviving offspring. For former golf pro Brian Floriani, it led to a change of course. He went from walking the greens with adults to sitting down and reading books with kids. Brian founded Bernie's Book Bank, a non-profit group whose mission is to significantly increase book ownership among at-risk infants, toddlers, and school-age children.

The organization is named in honor of Brian's father Dr. Bernard P. Floriani, a self-made man who began life as the son of a coal miner in a house without running water. He may not have had much, but he did have access to books and the opportunity for a good education. "Big Bernie" went to college on a basketball scholarship, achieved a bachelor's, a master's, and a doctorate degree in reading education, and spent his entire professional life promoting literacy.

When he suddenly died in 2005, Brian, who was a lead instructor for Golf Digest Schools in Lake Tahoe and West Palm Beach, was inspired to do something different with his life: something more meaningful, something that would have an impact on the world, such as following in his father's footsteps.

Brian began working as a reading paraprofessional for Shiloh Park Elementary in Zion, Illinois. He spent every day tutoring struggling readers. It wasn't long, though, before he wanted to do more. He wanted to make a bigger impact than he could by helping each child individually at the elementary school level; he wanted to help the tens of thousands of kids who enter the school system every year struggling to read.

From his time as a reading paraprofessional, he'd come to understand what his father had always known: that reading is the single most important skill a child needs in order to contribute and function competently within our society. Furthermore, he realized that all these children lacking reading skills probably could have been reading ready if they had been provided access to books at home before entering kindergarten. That's when he founded Bernie's Book Bank, an organization that would deliver access to books and the knowledge with them.

He launched in December 2009, working out of the garage of his home. In his first 12 months, he collected, processed, and distributed 140,000 children's books. In his second year, he distributed 350,000 books. By the end of 2012, the number was up to one million and 2017 was projected to hit a staggering 10 million. Its *books for a better life* purpose continues to spur on efforts.

Brian, who works as the non-profit's executive director, told us, "We're guaranteed the pursuit of happiness in this country, but it's predicated on whom you know and what you know. If you're in at at-risk community, you really only have one of these cards—the knowledge card—so we want to make sure those children are as prepared for learning and success as possible."

Bernie's Book Bank does this by collecting new and gently used books from their donors. It sorts the books into age-appropriate groups, and places a variety of six into bags that are delivered to the children via the school district's and federal government's Women, Infants, and Children (WIC) partners in the Chicagoland area. In one year, each child receives a total of 12 quality books to take home and call their own. Currently, more than 250,000 children a year are being helped via an army of 25,000 volunteers. The group has come a long way since it started in Brian's garage.

The non-profit organization claims, "Working together, we are transforming the educational journey of thousands of at-risk children by providing them the tools they need to become successful readers. Moving children from poverty to gaining knowledge through reading enables a legitimate pursuit of happiness. We believe that books and reading are both the vehicle and the road to a better life."[224]

This is the kind of impact that will be felt for generations to come; a legacy left from father to his son.

***

---

[224] Brian Floriani (Founder of Bernie's Book Bank) in discussion with the author, January 2017.

Company: Pantheon Enterprises

Location: Phoenix, Arizona

Business/Organization: Chemical manufacturer

Purpose: Innovate responsibly through Conscious Chemistry™ to sustain better life for people and our planet

Forbes magazine dubbed her the "Toxic Avenger." She's Laura Roberts, CEO of Pantheon Enterprises, who is fighting to protect our planet by shattering the myth that "safe" chemical technologies are more expensive, less effective, and harder to implement. An everyday hero, she found her purpose through a family tragedy and a chemical manufacturing company whose products are used by governments, commercial enterprises, and consumers who want to promote human health and safety, protect ecosystems and environments, and improve working conditions.

Laura told us, "We want to create public awareness of this giant uncontrolled experiment we're conducting on Earth, where we spew out tens of thousands of new molecules every year, with not enough regard to toxicity. We just continue to hope that this huge pool of chemistry we're concocting is not going to harm us, and that's got to change."

And Laura is leading the charge for change. Science and technology have added great value to our collective well-being, she says, but many of the chemicals that have been created over the last few centuries have had unintended negative consequences. "At Pantheon, we have chosen to be a catalyst for positive transformational change in the chemical industry by creating formulas, products, and solutions to sustain better life," she says. Pantheon calls it "Conscious Chemistry," a trademarked term for a set of rigorous standards developed to ensure their chemical formulations are both safe and effective.

Laura knew from an early age that she wanted to make a difference in the world, but it took some time for her to figure out how to do that.

Growing up in the 80s, she watched her dad try new things at the chemical company he and her mother founded. Even though her dad didn't come from the chemical world, he was something of a mad chemist who loved experimenting with different ways of mixing things and creating environmentally safe products.

Her father's entrepreneurial spirit made an impression on Laura, but when it was time for her to choose a career, she decided she wanted to be a teacher. She wanted to do good for the world and was passionate about what we now call sustainability. At the time, Laura was disappointed with Corporate America because she thought it was taking advantage of the ecosystem, so she chose to become a teacher and teach sustainability in the classroom.

With the help of independent investors and three other founders who believed in the company's ideals and the expanded vision, the business transformed itself into a brand-new company, and Pantheon Enterprises was born. For Laura, she finally had a chance to start a conversation about how chemistry was done in the world and how they could design chemicals that could make the world a better place to live. Back then, no one was talking about green chemistry seriously; Pantheon was one of the earliest. It was going green before it was cool.

In her industry, Laura believes the impact on humanity should be measured by the reduction in the number of chemicals being used in the world and by the reduction in the number of people getting sick from toxic chemicals. One way Pantheon measures its own impact is the work they've done with the aerospace industry. For years, Pantheon encouraged companies to stop using surface pre-treatments and processes containing hexavalent chromium, a toxic chemical that threatens the health and safety of anyone exposed to it. Finally, the industry listened, and switched to using Pantheon's flagship and more environmentally friendly product, PreKote.

Laura also realized she had to change the way she hired members of the

Tribe. She realized she had to stop thinking that if she hired people who simply had the right résumé, magic would happen. She realized it was emotional intelligence, not IQ, which was needed. So, Pantheon changed the way it interviewed prospective employees to discover more about their life purpose. They started asking job seekers questions such as, "What's important to you?" and "What's your story when you're 80?" and "What do you care about in the world?" Laura's willingness to invest more in the interview process and dig deeper paid off. Beyond that, Laura wants to invest in the future by changing the conversation today: "Hopefully, 20 years from now, we can be one of many companies that are making a real significant impact. My goal is to be part of a wave of people who continue the conversation and build upon it."

The story of Laura and Pantheon Enterprises is a compelling one. We can't all take on the worthy task of saving humanity from toxic chemicals, but whatever our field of endeavor, with a willingness to change and a commitment to being a force for good, we can make a positive difference.[225]

Not all superheros wear capes.

***

---

[225] Laura Roberts (CEO of Pantheon Enterprises) in discussion with the author, December 2016.

Company: CASE Construction Equipment (A CNH Industrial Brand)

Location: Racine, Wisconsin

Business/Organization: Manufacturer

Purpose: We believe in building communities

The CASE Construction Equipment journey to finding purpose began when a former colleague approached Senior Marketing Director Athena Campos seeking sponsorship. The former business associate, an author and infrastructure expert, intended to tour the U.S. in his rusty 1957 Hudson. His goal: to build awareness of the crumbling infrastructure at a time when the anemic Federal budget had led to tragedies—most recently the Minneapolis River bridge collapse that killed 13 people and injured 145.

Athena says, "We agreed to be the sponsor, but simply handing over a check didn't seem to be enough or very authentic." So, she and her team rolled up their sleeves and built an entire plan around the idea. They created and trademarked a cause marketing platform that CASE would own and nurture called "Dire States."

The Hudson tour to build awareness of the issue was the launching pad for future CASE Dire States initiatives, including support for local and state infrastructure bills in Texas, Pennsylvania, Illinois, and Wisconsin, to name a few. And that cause evolved into further advocacy and action through Dire States grant programs launched in 2016.

Through Dire States, CASE agreed to help the U.S. Wildlife Refuge with a land-clearing project that involved a non-profit disaster relief organization called Team Rubicon (also featured in Tuthill Corporation's case study). That relationship also flourished into additional community building (and rebuilding) opportunities, as well as an ability to help veterans identify new career opportunities as equipment operators.

It's a significant step for a company with a long and respected history. An entrepreneur in the industrial revolution era, Jerome Increase Case, founded the company in 1842 to make farming more efficient. He started by designing and selling threshers through the JI Case Threshing Machine Company of Racine, Wisconsin.

Today, CASE Construction is a global full-line provider, and part of a $2.4 Billion dollar CNH Industrial construction business worldwide. It sells light- to full-size construction equipment under 12 different product lines in North America and boasts about $2.3 billion in construction equipment revenues. CNH Industrial, reported worldwide revenues of about $24 billion (in 2016) and 64,000 employees.

CASE is still in the process of discovering and developing its corporate purpose, which it feels is extremely important because it allows the company to differentiate itself and attract and retain talent at a time of struggle for the agricultural and construction industries.

According to Athena, "It started as a desire to provide purpose to my career as a marketer and my team as a whole. I've always had a servant's heart and a passion to help others, but as the breadwinner of my family, I didn't have the luxury of staying home and volunteering or even working for nonprofits. I quickly realized, however, that by thinking a little creatively about our roles as marketers and the brand stories we tell, we were able to give back to the community in a way that was still serving all stakeholders—including investors. In fact, our goodwill resulted in incremental brand consideration and sales."

Adds Athena, "Everybody wins. I have a sense of personal fulfillment in my role. I love my job! How many people can say that today? It helps energize my team…they, too, have servants hearts and they're delivering better marketing ideas and stories as a result. I believe under our (proposed) purpose of, "Building community," we have the potential to help small operators grow by better managing their telematics data and finding infrastructure funding in their communities. I see us focusing on helping entrepreneurs expand."

While CASE shares both internally and externally all the good its done for the community and the brand, Athena says the company isn't yet formally discussing its purpose and hasn't put it into a framework. Right now, it's being cultivated in the marketing organization at Case Construction North America.

Athena says, "This book interview provided the data and context (and confidence) for me to build a business case and take it to the executive team. That's in the works."[226]

We're happy to have been of assistance and can't wait to see what a purpose transformation brings!

***

---

[226] Athena Campos (Senior Marketing Director at CASE Construction Equipment) in discussion with the author, February 2017.

196

Company: Payline Data

Location: Chicago, Illinois

Business/Organization: Financial services

Purpose: To positively impact our customers and make the world a better place

Before there was Payline, there was Purpose. Co-founders Jeff Shea (CEO) and Steve Blentlinger (Chief Strategy Officer) conceptualized their purpose for Payline Data even before they launched the fast-growing payment processing company in 2010.

Steve told us, "Our culture is a reflection of our purpose and has been from day one. We realized in our own lives, 'Why we work determines how well we work.' Jeff and I always talked about 'What is our Why?' We started Payline using this question to develop the blueprint for the company foundation." With that, they established:

- Their *Why*: "Everything we do, we believe it must create a positive impact."

- Their *How*: "We make a Positive Impact by enabling innovative software and products to improve business, and share our time and resources with those in need."

- Their *What*: "We just happen to be in the payments industry."

Then, they established their Core Values:

- *Passion*: Be excellent at what you do. Invest the time, resources, and abilities to achieve above-average results.

- *Purpose*: Focus on creating exceptional customer experiences all the time! (This, they say, holds true at every contact point: sales, customer service, technical assistance, product development, etc.)

- *Positive Impact*: Volunteer time and abilities and donate financially to those in need. Many members of their Tribe wear shirts bearing the message "Be the Positive Impact."

According to Steve, "These founding principles drive clear results, which we can measure to ensure we are achieving the Positive Impact: one, we continuously create opportunities for our employees to grow and our clients to achieve goals they could not otherwise achieve without our assistance. And: two, donation of time, talents, and resources to give back to those in need."

While giving back has always been a Payline core purpose, the company revitalized its mission in January 2017 with its "Payline Giving" program. Each employee is given the opportunity to attend a charity event once a month or to volunteer on a regular basis. Payline encourages its team to participate by providing three paid days off to do volunteer work.[227]

Inbound Marketing Manager Renee Kovalcheck told us, "Our company culture follows the notion of our Why. We believe strongly in investing in our employees and giving them opportunities to grow both in the technical aspects of their jobs and overall as a well-rounded professional."

She adds, "We like to describe our culture as caring, hip, youthful, and on the cutting-edge of the industry. We support each other immensely in having company goals and departmental goals."[228]

Payline's Why is central to its existence. As Senior Vice President of Revenue, Carlton van Putten, puts it, "Re-humanizing business and the workplace is disruptive and advantageous because it's not about us, it's about the people that work here and the potential to give back to those in need. It's unique and resonates with a younger generation of consumers. While tech and business model innovations can be replicated, culture cannot. Our culture has attracted a certain caliber of employees who are looking for purpose and meaning in their work beyond just receiving a

---

[227] Steve Blentlinger (Co-founder and Chief Strategy Officer at Payline) in discussion with the author, 2016-2017.
[228] Renee Kovalcheck (Inbound Marketing Manager at Payline Data) in discussion with the author, 2016-2017.

paycheck."[229]

Payline's purpose-driven approach definitely gets results. Payline was ranked #208 and #363 on the prestigious *Inc. 500* list of fastest-growing companies in the U.S. in 2016 and 2017, respectively. The company has also been nationally recognized as #15 on the list of privately held financial services businesses and the eighth fastest growing in the Chicago market. In hard numbers, that means three-year sales growth of 1,866 percent and $5 million in revenue in 2015.

Payline says, "We have attracted top talent to work with us to continue to help us reach the next level." And as far as their clients are concerned: "Unlike other payment vendors who only care about what's on their bottom line, we care about what's on our customers' horizon."

Steve and Jeff were far-sighted when they imagined Payline and have been rewarded by seeing the Impact they have already been able to make.

Purpose has definitely paid off for Payline!

***

---

[229] Carlton van Putten (Senior Vice President of Revenue at Payline Data) in discussion with the author, 2016-2017.

Company: Chicago Bar Company, LLC/RXBAR (A Kellogg's Company)

Location: Chicago, Illinois

Business/Organization: Protein bar manufacturer

Purpose: No B.S. life

RXBAR is serious when it says it takes a no B.S. approach to business. It's right there—upfront—on the labels of the protein bars this rapidly growing company manufactures. Look at its Chocolate Sea Salt Bar, for example. It spells out the key ingredients in big type like this:

3 Egg Whites

6 Almonds

4 Cashews

2 Dates

No B.S.

Then consider the detailed Nutrition Facts statement on the back and you'll find it is simplicity itself. None of those complicated, chemically sounding unpronounceable ingredients you see on most products. The RXBAR reflects the no-nonsense attitude of the company.

The business is founded on transparency and authenticity. It knows what its belief is. As CEO and co-founder Peter Rahal puts it, "You're only here for a little amount of time. So being direct, honest, and transparent can lead to a better life. Hold yourself accountable. Nothing misleading."

The company is becoming a big player in the nutrition bar market. You'll find the bars on the shelves of many major supermarkets. But part of the company passion is making sure that no matter how big they get, they never forget their roots. That's part of being authentic.

And what does that mean in reality? It means that new recruits, as part of a seven-week onboarding process, get the opportunity to make the bars by hand—just like when the company started.

According to Peter, "This drives business empathy and helps our team members understand how much goes into making the product, as well as insight into the manufacturing and R&D process."[230]

And that's no B.S.

***

---

[230] Peter Rahal (CEO and Co-founder of RXBAR) in discussion with the author, July 2016.

Company: Shure Incorporated

Location: Headquarters in Niles, Illinois; 26 locations worldwide

Business/Organization: Manufacturer of professional audio products

Purpose: The most trusted audio brand worldwide

In today's fast-paced world, people often change *careers* several times—never mind *jobs*. A job that exists today may not even exist 10 years from now. That's why Shure Incorporated's ability to keep quality employees year after year is all the more remarkable. According to Michael Pettersen, Shure's Director of Corporate History, "Associates stay at Shure their entire careers. As of August 2017, my 41 years of service only ranks as number 11 in seniority."

Why is that? How does the company inspire such loyalty and commitment? Probably because the company—founded in 1925 by S.N. Shure—has never wavered from the fundamental principles he laid down, much of it based on the Judaica teachings of, "Ethics of the Fathers."

Shure, which began as a distributor (via catalog) of radio parts, now primarily sells professional wireless microphones, wired microphones, related audio devices, and earphones.

Its stated mission is to be *the most trusted audio brand worldwide*. "Service to others. Ethics. Trust."

When you hear a company historian use words like these before saying anything else, you truly appreciate the foundation on which the business has been built, and how it has been able to expand to 24 locations worldwide. You can tell a business takes its purpose seriously when you hear it has covered the topic extensively in a two-volume corporate history titled, *Shure: Sound People, Products, and Values*.

Quality and reliability of products are the principal factors in every decision the company makes, and while the methods of doing business change constantly based on market demands and innovations, the fundamental ethics remain inflexible.

Michael told us, "For 41 years, I have traveled the world representing Shure. In every country, I hear the same story: 'I love Shure. Shure makes products that are always reliable and of the highest quality. You are welcome anytime to visit my company...my business...my home...my recording studio...my theater.'" Adds Michael, "The products 'speak for themselves' and the way we treat customers every day speaks volumes about our core values."

Shure's products sure do speak for themselves. The first-floor exhibit at company headquarters highlights its most popular products—and its Archive has about 3,000, one of every major product made since 1932. The company estimates that at least 98 percent still operate properly. Some customers have returned products—but not for the reason you might think. Shure's returns are from people who say they are, "Sending them back home." Some are mics that were used by dad or granddad, and some that had been abused beyond belief were sent back because the customers were so astonished by their durability.

Other customers have shown their commitment to Shure by having their favorite mic tattooed on their bodies. You can find an amazing gallery of colorful artwork if you Google "Shure tattoos."

Shure's commitment to sharing begins internally. Its *Shure Shots* publication has been published since 1942; today there are also daily messages on the company's intranet. Associates live and breathe the Shure philosophy through ongoing training and core value workshops.

No wonder the company, after 92 years in business, is, as S. N. Shure once said, heading "Upward, ever upward." We look forward to seeing Shure celebrate its 100th anniversary while still honoring the following core values established at its inception.

Core Values

Here's what Shure believes keeps the company on the up and up.

THE **SCIENCE** OF STORY

- As a Company and as individuals, we are ethical, honest, and fair in dealing with associates, customers, and suppliers.

- We manufacture products of unmatched quality, reliability, and durability.

- Shure Associates show respect for one another in all circumstances.

- Shure is a good corporate citizen, neighbor, and employer.[231]

Shure—a sound company, for sure.

***

---

[231] Michael Pettersen (Director of Corporate History at Shure Incorporated) in discussion with the author, March 2017.

Company: JetBlue

Location: Long Island City, New York; 101 cities nationwide

Business/Organization: Airline

Purpose: Inspiring humanity

When JetBlue got off the ground in the year 2000, its mission was to bring humanity back to air travel. It was a time when the traveling public was totally disenchanted with the airline experience. On the whole, you might ask, is it much better today? Passengers back then were dismayed with the way they were treated at airports and on planes. Air travel was tedious and painful. Service was lackluster. And, to rub salt in the wound, prices were sky high!

Enter JetBlue with the bold mission to bring humanity back to air travel by creating an airline with friendly crewmembers and lower fares, an airline that you actually wanted to fly. As it moved into its second decade of operation, JetBlue felt it had accomplished that mission. It had added competition to many markets that were not only underserved, but also where travelers previously were hit with outrageous ticket costs. It had helped lower fares, and it had done it all with award-winning service.

It was time for a purpose refresh. The company needed to discover a soaring new purpose. It became somewhat grander: *inspiring humanity.* This encompassed its approach in the air, and on the ground, and also with an eye toward long-term environmental planning and social responsibility, always asking the question: How are we leaving the planet in better shape for future generations?

It begins, says JetBlue, with its people. Tamara Young, Manager of Corporate Communications, told us, "We are a values-based company. Our crewmembers operate with safety, caring, integrity, passion, and fun in mind. These values guide our decisions as crewmembers, in the community, and as a company."[232]

Stop right there. When you hear the word "crewmember," you probably think of the pilots and the flight attendants. But JetBlue uses the term to describe employees at all levels within its workforce of 21,000 people. JetBlue has dropped the "employee" moniker because it says it doesn't accurately describe the passionate individuals who make up their workforce.

"When we use the word crewmember, it's because everybody is a crewmember," Marty St. George, EVP, Commercial and Planning, told us. "We've created a culture where there's a direct relationship between our crewmembers and our leadership. It is very much an egalitarian society."[233]

It's also a way of identifying the right kind of people to join such a purpose-driven company. As Mike Elliott, EVP, People, told us, "When I talk to folks about our culture, I view it as the personality of the company. As we continue to grow we need to hire the right people...so that every crewmember has ownership in sustaining our culture."[234]

JetBlue's unique culture begins from within on the crewmember's first day at JetBlue University, the airline's training campus in Orlando, Florida. JetBlue hosts an orientation every two weeks where the CEO and/ or C-Suite executives usually greet each incoming class so they are the first faces that new crewmembers see and meet.

The new arrivals soon learn that service is an integral part of JetBlue's brand. Everyone, from the top executives down, participates in the company's corporate social responsibility and volunteer programs, inspiring crewmembers to give back to customers and the communities they serve.

Among the highlights of JetBlue's volunteerism, service and social

---

[232] Tamara Young (Manager of Corporate Communications at JetBlue) in discussion with the author, November 2016.
[233] Marty St. George (EVP, Commercial and Planning at JetBlue) in discussion with the author, November 2016.
[234] Mike Elliott (EVP, People at JetBlue) in discussion with the author, November 2016.

responsibility:

- 500,000+ hours of service volunteered by crewmembers since 2011.

- Close to 2 billion pounds of greenhouse gas emissions offset in eight years as a result of a partnership with CarbonFund.org.

- Nearly $3 million worth of books donated to kids who need them the most through the award-winning Soar with Reading initiative.

- 7 playgrounds built across the country, thanks to a partnership with KaBOOM!

Frequent communication is vital in promoting these programs and making crewmembers aware of other corporate developments. JetBlue leadership works hard to keep in touch with its crewmembers in a variety of ways, including a daily newsletter. Everyone can participate in "HelloJetBlue," a personalized intranet experience. JetBlue also believes in keeping it real. When you see someone in an ad wearing a JetBlue uniform, it's a real crewmember. When you see a customer, it's a real customer. They're not actors.

Adds Tamara, "Our core business is about connection. We connect people, whether it's family, friends, or colleagues. And we hire based on attitude versus aptitude. We like to say if JetBlue were a person, people would want to be our friend. Our crewmembers *are* JetBlue. This is important to our culture and gives a sense of pride."

While it's no longer a start-up, JetBlue continues to disrupt the industry, and takes pride in being "definitely different than legacy airlines." For a high-flying company, it sure does have a down-to-earth attitude.

***

Company: Baird & Warner

Location: Chicago, Illinois

Business/Organization: Real estate services

Purpose: Real estate made easier

On March 28, 1855, Baird & Warner made its debut in the real estate market with its first transaction—a whopping $5,000 mortgage loan. Today, more than 160 years later, the Chicago-based firm boasts total sales of over $8 billion and is represented by more than 2,300 real estate brokers. Why is it such a dominant force in Chicagoland real estate?

It's probably got something to do with the fact that, as the company puts it, "We are the market's most progressive company, with a long-standing heartfelt commitment to the principles of fair housing and diversity, driven by five generations of independent local family ownership. This heritage empowers us to reinvent our company and capabilities to meet the evolving needs of the people we serve."

They add, "Baird & Warner continuously seeks out the most promising innovations as we develop new solutions and services for our clients and broker associates—that's how the nation's oldest real estate company remains so young and relevant."

Baird & Warner offers consumers a variety of services, whether you're buying or selling a home, including title insurance and, just like it did in 1855, handling your need for a mortgage.

Its latest innovation, the purpose statement of *making real estate easier (for everyone)*, developed from extensive research among its stakeholders and customer base as it set out, "Looking for a unique, tangible, fact-based 'why' to own," Peter Papakyriacou, Vice President of Marketing and Communications, told us.

According to Peter, "People told us they see real estate transactions as confusing, stressful, and complicated. So we have made the commitment across all business units and across all levels of management that anything we work on, service or tool we purchase, strategy we devise, process we implement, will have to pass through the filter of 'does it make it easier?'"

The adoption of the "easier" purpose, says Peter, has been truly remarkable: "It is becoming our raison d'être. It has resonated at the most foundational level. It is the right thing to do, creating a unifying focus for our company to build upon." It gets results, too. Within the first month of launching its "easier" social strategy, Baird & Warner experienced a 53 percent increase in engagement and 43 percent increase in followers on Facebook.

Baird & Warner knows that success begins at home. That's why it has put a lot of effort into creating a thriving and positive work environment, so much so, that in 2016, the firm earned its fifth consecutive Top Workplace award from the *Chicago Tribune*.[235]

According to Steve Baird, President and CEO, "Behind every great company is a culture created by the professionals who are living its experiences and sharing the stories that define it. We are a team of like-minded but unique individuals working together to make it easier for homebuyers and sellers across Chicagoland to achieve their real estate dreams. By celebrating the exceptional strengths and empowering our broker associates and employees to be the best they can be, we create something extraordinary. Something impactful."

Being a Top Workplace five years running, says Steve, is about doing things the right way: "It means creating a culture of open doors and open minds that empowers us to grow as individuals and thrive as a company. I firmly believe that by working together, we are building a solid foundation for the future."[236]

Real estate with a solid foundation—now there's a thought.

***

---

[235] Peter Papakyriacou (Vice President of Marketing and Communications at Baird & Warner) in discussion with the author, July 2016.

[236] Steve Baird (President and CEO at Baird & Warner) in discussion with the author, July 2016.

Company: Bucketfeet

Location: Chicago, Illinois

Business/Organization: Shoe company

Purpose: Creating a brighter world

In 2008, Raaja Nemani quit his job and set off to backpack around the world. In Argentina, while volunteering, he met Aaron Firestein, an artist living in Buenos Aires, and was blown away by Aaron's creativity of turning footwear into works of art.

Before Raaja left Argentina, Aaron gave him a pair of hand-designed canvas sneakers inspired by the city blocks of Buenos Aires. Invariably, no matter where Raaja went, the shoes were a huge talking point—they were always the catalyst for conversations with strangers. Throughout the remainder of Raaja's journey, the pair of shoes sparked hundreds of conversations across six continents with people of all races, religions, genders, and cultures.

Raaja had an "aha moment." What a terrific way to help forge a more connected world—a unique way through footwear. Raaja got back in touch with Aaron and two years later they joined forces to launch Bucketfeet, a company that sells artist-designed footwear.

Bucketfeet empowers artists to share their stories and perspectives using the universal language of art and a shoe as their canvas. Bucketfeet's Artist Network has grown from one (Aaron) to more than 40,000 in more than 120 countries. They range from graphic designers and fine artists to street artists, graffiti artists, photographers, students, and everything in-between. Once they began to Express their message, their Tribe ran with it and expressed it over and over again.

The way it works is that anyone can register to be a Bucketfeet artist and submit artwork via the company's online platform. An in-house team evaluates each submission and selects the strongest designs, which are then prepped for release. In its on-demand supply chain, Bucketfeet hand-makes every pair of shoes at the time of order and delivers within 10 days.

It's a direct-to-consumer brand that's disrupting the $300-billion shoe industry's traditional marketing cycle.

Artists receive a royalty for every pair of shoes sold. Since launch, over $500,000 has been given back to the artist community. Says Bucketfeet, "Every shoe is a collaboration—an artist designs every pair of shoes we produce, and every pair of shoes tells a different story."

Bucketfeet believes in giving back, and in working with organizations that not only share its worldview, but also have impactful stories to share. Consumers can ignite conversations and show their support for causes that matter to them by purchasing shoes that visibly and artistically represent their cause. And Bucketfeet certainly walks its talk. During the 2016 holiday season, the company took part in (RED) SHOPATHON to support the fight against AIDS with a contribution that can provide over 8,000 days of life-saving medication. Also on the health front, it has teamed up with national non-profit group Bright Pink in their mission to prevent breast and ovarian cancer in young women. Every pair of specially designed shoes enables four women to get educated about breast and ovarian cancer prevention.

In the natural world, Bucketfeet has partnered with the Lonely Whale Foundation to launch a limited-edition shoe that promotes dialogue about the foundation's dedication to bringing people closer to the world's oceans through education and awareness, inspiring empathy and action for ocean health and the well-being of marine wildlife.

Says Bucketfeet co-founder and CEO Raaja Nemani, "You can say you believe something, but you have to live it. Following a North Star and having a cohesive brand statement is important for building trust for consumers and artists. We came up with our purpose statement of *creating a brighter world* as a play on words, as most of the footwear is bright and colorful. And we want the world to be a brighter place in every sense of the word. If we all feel more connected, it makes the world a better place."[237]

That's what Bucketfeet is doing—one shoe and one step at a time.

---

[237] Raaja Nemani (Co-founder and CEO) in discussion with the author, February 2017.

Bibliography

Abston PhD, Kristie A. and Virginia W. Kupritz PhD. "Employees as customers: Exploring service climate, employee patronage, and turnover." *Performance Improvement Quarterly* 23, no. 4 (2011): 7-26.

Adamson, Allen. "Culture Eats Brand Strategy For Lunch At FedEx." *Forbes*, March 10, 2017. https://www.forbes.com/sites/allenadamson/2017/03/10/culture-eats-brand-strategy-for- lunch-at-fedex/#16c325031863.

Aflac."Aflac Corporate Social Responsibility Survey Fact Sheet." Last modified November 16, 2015. Accessed November 28, 2017. https://www.philanthropy.com/items/biz/pdf/AflacCorporateSocialResponsibility.pdf.

Arby's. "Who We Are and What We Do." https://arbys.com/about.

ARCA. "Our History." https://arca.com/company/history.

Baer, Drake. "Here's What Google Teaches employees In Its 'Search Inside Yourself' Course." *Business Insider*, August 5, 2014. http://www.businessinsider.com/search-inside-yourself-googles-life-changing-mindfulness-course-2014-8.

Baer, Drake. "How Changing One Habit Helped Quintuple Alcoa's Income." *Business Insider*, April 9, 2014. http://www.businessinsider.com/how-changing-one-habit-quintupled-alcoas-income-2014-4.

Baldoni, John. "Employee Engagement Does More than Boost Productivity." *Harvard Business Review*, July 4, 2013. https://hbr.org/2013/07/employee-engagement-does-more.

Beer, Jeff. "How General Electric Created the Hit Science-Fiction Podcast 'The Message.'" *Fast Company*, November 25, 2015. https://www.fastcompany.com/3053982/how-general-electric-created-the-hit-science-fiction-podcast-the-message.

Beer, Michael, Magnus Finnström, and Derek Schrader. "Why Leadership Training Fails - and What to Do about It." *Harvard Business Review*, October 2016. https://hbr.org/2016/10/why-leadership-training-fails-and-what-to-do-about-it.

Bersin, Josh. "Learning Management Systems: Are They Coming To An End?" Deloitte. January 2017. Accessed November 28, 2017. https://www.edcast.com/corp/wp-content/uploads/2017/01/2017_01_LMS_EDCAST_2.1c.pdf.

Bonetto, Lauren. "56 Percent of Americans Stop Buying from Brands They Believe Are Unethical." *Mintel*. November 18, 2015. Accessed November 28, 2017. http://www.mintel.com/press-centre/social-and-lifestyle/56-of-americans-stop-buying-from-brands-they-believe-are-unethical.

Blaustein Clancy Financial Group of Wells Fargo. "Our Firm." http://www.blausteinclancy.wfadv.com/Our-Firm.2.htm.

Bluestein, Adam. "How to Tell Your Company's Story." *Inc Magazine*, February 2014. https://www.inc.com/magazine/201402/adam-bluestein/sara-blakely-how-i-got-started.html.

Brown, Aleksa. "Company Culture: Gathering Around the Table at Eatsy." *Etsy Journal*, November 28, 2012. https://blog.etsy.com/en/gathering-around-the-table-at-eatsy/.

Bruell, Alexandra. "Tech Company Takes Top Prize in Cannes Pharma Category as Health Sees New Entrants." *AdAge*, June 18, 2016. http://adage.com/article/agency-news/tech-company-takes-top-prize-cannes-lions-pharma-category/304578/.

Bureau of Labor Statistics. "Business Employment Dynamics Summary." Last modified January 26, 2018. https://www.bls.gov/news.release/cewbd.nr0.htm.

Calori, Roland and Philippe Sarnin. "Corporate Culture and Economic Performance: A French Study." *Organization Studies* 12, no. 1 (1991): 49-74.

Collins, Jim, and Jerry I. Porras. "Building Your Company's Vision." *Harvard Business Review*, September-October 1996. http://www.hbr.org/1996/09/building-your-companys-vision.

Costly, Andrew. "Bill of Rights in Action." *Constitutional Rights Foundation.* Spring 2003. Accessed November 28, 2017. http://www.crf-usa.org/bill-of-rights-in-action/bria-19-2-b-social-darwinism-and-american-laissez-faire-capitalism.html.

Cowley, Stacy. "'Lions Hunting Zebras': Ex-Wells Fargo Bankers Describe Abuses." *The New York Times.* October 20, 2016. http://www.nytimes.com/2016/10/21/business/dealbook/lions-hunting-zebras-ex-wells-fargo-bankers-describe-abuses.html.

Charron, Todd. "Scaling Agile at Spotify: An Interview with Henrik Kniberg." *InfoQ*, April 9, 2013.https://www.infoq.com/news/2013/04/scaling-agile-spotify-kniberg.

Crabtree, Steve. "Worldwide, 13 percent of Employees Are Engaged at Work." *Gallup News*, October 8, 2013. http://news.gallup.com/poll/165269/worldwide-employees-engaged-work.aspx.

Curtis, Valerie A., Lisa O. Danquah, and Robert V. Aunger. "Planned, motivated and habitual hygiene behaviour: an eleven country review." *Health Education Research* 24, no. 4 (March 2009): 655-673.

"Danish Employees Are the Happiest in the EU." *Copenhagen Capacity*, May 5, 2014. http://www.copcap.com/newslist/2014/danish-employees-are-the-happiest-in-the-eu.

Dannen, Chris. "Inside gitHub's Super-Lean Management Straetgy-And How It Drives Innovation." *Fast Company*, October 18, 2013. https://www.fastcompany.com/3020181/inside-githubs-super-lean-management- strategy-

and-how-it-drives-innovation.

Dignan, Aaron. "If the Answer Is 'It's Just Policy,' You're F*cked." *Medium*. November 07, 2015. https://medium.com/the-ready/if-the-answer-is-it-s-just-policy-you-re-fucked-375d1ced3ec2.

Dignan, Aaron. "The Last Re-Org You'll Ever Do." *Medium*, December 15, 2013. https://medium.com/the-ready/the-last-re-org-youll-ever-do-f19160f61500.

Dillan. "The Power of Habit Summary." *Deconstructing Excellence*, May 26, 2015. http://www.deconstructingexcellence.com/the-power-of-habit-summary/.

Duhigg, Charles. "How 'Keystone Habits' Transformed a Corporation." *HuffPost*, February 27, 2012. https://www.huffingtonpost.com/charles-duhigg/the-power-of-habit_b_1304550.html.

Edwards, Vanessa Van. Captivate: *The Science of Succeeding with People*. New York: Portfolio/Penguin, 2017.

Elenburg, Dennis. Book review: "Who Says Elephants Can't Dance?" IBM. May 15, 2003. Accessed November 28, 2017. https://www.ibm.com/developerworks/rational/library/2071.html.

Engel, Pamela. "Here's The Text Message Malaysia Airlines Sent To The Families Of The Lost Passengers." *Business Insider*, March 24, 2014. http://www.businessinsider.com/malaysia-airlines-text-message-to-families-2014-3.

English Oxford Living Dictionaries. Online ed., "expression."

English Oxford Living Dictionaries. Online ed., "mindfulness."

English Oxford Living Dictionaries. Online ed., "tribe."

Everlane. "About." https://www.everlane.com/about.

EY Entrepreneurial Winning Women Conference. "Winning with Purpose." May 2016. Accessed November 28, 2017.http://www.ey.com/Publication/vwLUAssets/EY-purpose-led-organizations/$FILE/EY-purpose-led-organizations.pdf.

Eurich, Laura. "Pick Purpose, Not Passion." *Colorado Springs Independent*. May 1, 2013. https://www.csindy.com/coloradosprings/pick-purpose-not-passion/Content?oid=2666903.

Fowler, Susan. "Reflecting On One Very, Very Strange Year At Uber." *Susan Fowler*, February 19, 2017. https://www.susanjfowler.com/blog/2017/2/19/reflecting-on-one-very-strange-year-at-uber.

Frankl, Viktor. *Man's Search for Meaning*. Boston: Beacon Press, 2006.

"A Meaningful Job Linked to Higher Income and a Longer Life." *Association for Psychological Science*, January 3, 2017.https://www.psychologicalscience.org/news/minds-business/a-meaningful-job-linked-to-higher-income-and-a-longer-life.html#.WRbt_2jyvIU.

Fridman, Adam. "Do You Know Your Brand Identity? It Starts With Your Why." *Inc.*, February 2, 2016. https://www.inc.com/adam-fridman/do-you-know-your-brand-identity-it-s-start-with-your-why.html.

Fridman, Adam. "Empathy Makes Us Human - Connecting Audiences to Your

Brand's Story." *Inc.*, September 28, 2016. https://www.inc.com/adam-fridman/empathy-makes-us-human--connecting-audiences-to-your-brands-story.html.

Fridman, Adam. "How Your Purpose Answers Why Your Brand Exists." *Inc.*, October 13, 2016. https://www.inc.com/adam-fridman/how-your-purpose-answers-the-reason-for-why-your-brand-exists.html.

Fridman, Adam. "Transforming Life at Work: Inspiring Culture and Influencing Engagement Within the Workplace." *Inc.*, October 4, 2017. https://www.inc.com/adam-fridman/transforming-life-at-work-inspiring-culture-influencing-engagement-within-workplace.html.

Fridman, Adam. "5 Undeniable Reasons Brands Are a Reflection of Their Culture." *Inc.*, November 7, 2016. https://www.inc.com/adam-fridman/5-undeniable-reasons-brands-are-a-reflection-of-their-culture.html

Gallup. "The Engaged Workplace." Accessed November 28, 2017. http://www.gallup.com/services/190118/engagedworkplace.aspx?gclid=CIn487iJxM4CFdBZhgodhi4G2w.

Gilbert, Dr. Cyndi. "Neuroplasticity: your brain is playdough." *Cyndi Gilbert Naturopathic Doctor*, July 20, 2012. http://www.cyndigilbert.ca/neuroplasticity-your-brain-is-playdough/.

Global Wellness Institute. "The History of Wellness." https://www.globalwellnessinstitute.org/history-of-wellness/.

Gordon, George G. and Nancy DiTomaso. "Predicting Corporate Performance From Organizational Culture." *Journal of Management Studies* 29, no. 6 (1992): 783-798.

Griffith Foods. "Remembering Dean Griffith." http://www.griffithfoods.com/whoweare/Pages/Dean.aspx.

Guerrera, Francesco. "How 'Wall Street' changed Wall Street." *Financial Times*, September 24, 2010. https://www.ft.com/content/7e55442a-c76a-11df-aeb1-00144feab49a.

Guiso, Luigi, Paola Sapienza, and Luigi Zingales. "The Value of Corporate Culture." *Chicago Booth Research Paper*, no. 13-80 (November 2013). http://economics.mit.edu/files/9721.

Hampton, Debbie. "The Wolves Within." The Best Brain Possible, September 8, 2014. https://www.thebestbrainpossible.com/the-wolves-within/.

Hempel, Jessi. "Pixar University: Thinking Outside The Mouse." *SFGate*, June 4, 2003. http://www.sfgate.com/news/article/Pixar-University-Thinking-Outside-The-Mouse-2611923.php.

Hicks, Robin. "Why Thai Life Insurance ads are so consistently, tear-jerkingly brilliant." *Mumbrella Asia*, January 29, 2015. https://www.mumbrella.asia/2015/01/beyond-bright-shiny-things-real-issues-emerge-ces-marketers.

History. "Ford Factory Workers Get 40-hour Week." May 1, 2017. Accessed November 28, 2017. http://www.history.com/this-day-in-history/ford-factory-workers-get-40-hour-week.

Holacracy. "How It Works." https://www.holacracy.org/how-it-works/.

Hurst, Aaron. *The Purpose Economy*. Boise, ID: Elevate, a Russell Media company, 2014.

"A Meaningful Job Linked to Higher Income and a Longer Life." *Association for Psychological Science*. January 3, 2017. Accessed November 28, 2017. https://www.psychologicalscience.org/news/minds-business/a-meaningful-job-linked-to-higher-income-and-a-longer-life.html.

"IKEA Announces New 'Design by IKEA' Blog and 'Share Space' Photo-Sharing Website." *IKEA Corporate News*, August 16, 2011. http://www.ikea.com/us/en/about_ikea/newsitem/Blog_Share_Space_2011_release.

K, Alfred. "Monkeys Washing Potatoes." *Alfred*, April 2013. http://alfre.dk/monkeys-washing-potatoes/.

Kahn, William. "Psychological Conditions of Personal Engagement and Disengagement at Work." *Academy of Management Journal 33*, no. 4 (1990): 705.

Kantor, Jodi, and David Streitfeld. "Inside Amazon: Wrestling Big Ideas in a Bruising Workplace." *The New York Times*, August 15, 2015. https://www.nytimes.com/2015/08/16/technology/inside-amazon-wrestling-big-ideas-in-a-bruising-workplace.html.

Karvetski, Kerri. "7 Reasons Why This Gen X Nonprofit Marketer Has Fallen in Love with Slack." Kivi's Nonprofit Communications Blog, June 15, 2017. http://www.nonprofitmarketingguide.com/blog/2017/06/15/7-reasons-why-this-gen-x-nonprofit-marketer-has-fallen-in-love-with-slack/.

"'Keeping It Real' - Burson-Marsteller and IMD Business School Identify Drivers of Corporate Authenticity." *Burson-Marsteller*, April 14, 2015. http://www.burson-marsteller.com/news/press-release/keeping-it-real-burson-marsteller-and-imd-business-school-identify-drivers-of-corporate-authenticity/.

Kell, John. "This Is The New Way Nike Is Going After Women." *Fortune*, January 28, 2016. http://fortune.com/2016/01/28/nike-youtube-margot-lily/.

Kellogg's. "Our Vision & Purpose." http://www.kelloggcompany.com/en_US/our-vision-purpose.html.

Kenny, Graham. "Your Company's Purpose Is Not Its Vision, Mission, or Values" *Harvard Business Review*, September 3, 2014. https://hbr.org/2014/09/your-companys-purpose-is-not-its-vision-mission-or-values.

King, Jeff. "Only Conscious Capitalists Will Survive." *Forbes Magazine*. December 4, 2013, https://www.forbes.com/sites/onmarketing/2013/12/04/only-conscious-capitalists-will-survive/.

Korn Ferry Institute. "People on a mission." https://dsqapj1lakrkc.cloudfront.net/media/sidebar_downloads/Korn_Ferry_People_on_a_Mission_1219.pdf.

Kukk, Christopher. "Survival of the Fittest Has Evolved: Try Survival of the Kindest." *NBCNews.com*. March 8, 2017. Accessed November 28, 2017. https://www.nbcnews.com/better/relationships/survival-fittest-has-evolved-try-survival-kindest-n730196.

Kukk, Christopher. *The Compassionate Achiever*. New York, NY: HarperOne, 2017.

Lane, Sylvan. "Wells Fargo loses Better Business Bureau accreditation." *The Hill*, October 20, 2016. http://thehill.com/policy/finance/302080-wells-fargo-loses-better-business-bureau-accreditation.

"Latest News: Leading Corporations Believe in Corporate Purpose, according to the Burson-Marsteller/IMD Power of Purpose Study." *Burson Marsteller*, September 2, 2013. http://www.burson-marsteller.eu/latest-news/leading-corporations-believe-in-corporate-purpose-according-to-the-burson-marstellerimd-power-of-purpose-study/.

Lazauskas, Joe. "'We're a Media Company Now': Inside Marriott's Incredible Money-Making Content Studio." *Contently*, November 5, 2015. https://contently.com/strategist/2015/11/05/were-a-media-company-now-inside-marriotts-incredible-money-making-content-studio/.

Leider, Richard. The Power of Purpose. Oakland, CA: Berrett-Koehler Publishers, *Inc.*, 2015.

"Lincoln Park Zoo Unveils New National Conservation Efforts." *NBC 5 Chicago*, March 23, 2017. https://www.nbcchicago.com/news/local/Lincoln-Park-Zoo-Unveils-New-Conservation-Efforts-416984943.html.

Lings, Ian N. and Dr R. F. Brooks. "Implementing and Measuring the Effectiveness of Internal Marketing." *Journal of Marketing Management* 14, no. 4/5 (1998): 325-351.

Louisville Slugger. "Our History." http://www.slugger.com/en-us/our-history.

Lowery, Kate. "Conscious Capitalism: A New Book by our Co-Founder and Co-CEO, John Mackey." *Whole Foods Market Blog*. January 11, 2013. http://www.wholefoodsmarket.com/blog/conscious-capitalism-new-book-our-co-founder-and-co-ceo-john-mackey-0.

Maddox, Kate. "Deluxe Rolls Out 'Small Business Revolution' For Its Centennial."*AdAge*, April 21, 2015. http://adage.com/article/btob/deluxe-rolls-small-business-revolution-centennial/298174/.

Maio, Gregory R., and Victoria M. Esses. "The need for affect: Individual differences in the motivation to approach or avoid emotions." *Journal of Personality* 69, no. 4 (2001): 583-615.

Markel, Dr. Howard. "How the Tylenol murders of 1982 changed the way we consume medication." PBS News Hour, September 29, 2014. https://www.pbs.org/newshour/health/tylenol-murders-1982.

Maslow, Abraham. *The Farther Reaches of Human Nature*. New York: Penguin Group, 1993.

McCarthy, Niall. "Which Work Benefits Do Millennials Value Most? [Infographic]." *Forbes*, November 12, 2015. https://www.forbes.com/sites/niallmccarthy/2015/11/12/which-work-benefits-do-millennials-value-most-infographic/#2b90c03b34ff.

McClay, Rebecca. "Think Amazon's Bad? Here are 6 Companies with Worse Culture." *TheStreet*, August 17, 2015. https://www.thestreet.com/story/13257755/1/6-companies-with-worse-workplaces-than-amazon.html.

McGroarty, Beth "Global Wellness Institute Study: $3.4 Trillion Global Wellness market is Now Three Times Larger Than Worldwide Pharmaceutical Industry." *Global Wellness Institute*, 2014. https://www.globalwellnessinstitute.org/global-wellness-institute-study-34-trillion-global-wellness-market-is-now-three-times-larger-than-worldwide-pharmaceutical-industry.

McMurtry, Jeanette. "The Purpose-Driven Brand." *Target Marketing*, April 16, 2015. http://www.targetmarketingmag.com/post/the-purpose-driven-brand-why-it-matters-more-than-ever/all/.

Meglino, Bruce M., Elizabeth C. Ravlin, and Cheryl L. Adkins. "A Work Values Approach to Corporate Culture: A Field Test of the Value Congruence Process and Its Relationship to Individual Outcomes." *Journal of Applied Psychology* 70, no. 3 (December 2014): 424-432. https://www.researchgate.net/publication/232548618_A_Work_Values_Approach_to_Corporate_Culture_A_Field_Test_of_the_Value_Congruence_Process_and_Its_Relationship_to_Individual_Outcomes.

Michaels, Ed. The War for Talent. Boston: Massachusetts: Harvard Business School Publishing, 2001.

Mockenhaupt, Brian. "A State of Military Mind." *Pacific Standard*, June 18, 2012. https://psmag.com/social-justice/a-state-military-mind-42839.

Moore, Thomas. "The fight to save Tylenol (fortune, 1982)." *Fortune*, October 7, 2012. http://fortune.com/2012/10/07/the-fight-to-save-tylenol-fortune-1982/.

Nale, Stephen. "The 100 Greatest Steve Job Quotes." *Complex*, October 5, 2012, http://www.complex.com/pop-culture/2012/10/steve-jobs-quotes/focus-and-simpliity.

"PATAGONIA Launches '$20 Million & Change.'" *Mountain Blog Europe*, May 29, 2013. http://www.mountainblog.eu/patagonia-launches-20-million-change/.

Patterson, Malcolm, Peter Warr, and Michael West. "Organizational Climate and Company Productivity: The Role of Employee Affect and Employee Level." *Journal of Occupational and Organizational Psychology* 77, no. 2 (2004): 193-216.

Pinsker, Joe. "Corporations' Newest Hack: Meditation." *The Atlantic*, March 10, 2015. https://www.theatlantic.com/business/archive/2015/03/corporations-newest-productivty-hack-meditation/387286/.

Punjaisri, Khanyapuss and Alan Wilson. "The role of internal branding in the delivery of employee brand promise." *Journal of Brand Management* 15, no. 1 (2007): 57-70.

Purpose Guides Institute. "What Scientific Studies Show Purpose Gives You."

https://www.purposeguides.org/what-scientific-studies-show-purpose-gives-you/#.

Rozen, Dr. Michelle. "How to Create a Company Culture of Communication." *HuffPost*, July 18, 2016. https://www.huffingtonpost.com/michelle-rozen/how-to-create-a-company-c_b_11055992.html.

Ryan, Liz. "Ten Unmistakable Signs of a Toxic Culture." *Forbes*, October 20, 2016. https://www.forbes.com/sites/lizryan/2016/10/19/ten-unmistakable-signs-of-a-toxic-culture/2/#53da11297e42.

Saft, James. "Meditation and the art of investment." Reuters, April 17, 2013, http://blogs.reuters.com/james-saft/2013/04/17/meditation-and-the-art-of-investment/.

SaudiBeauty. "Introducing Clinique's Editorial Platform...The Wink." *SaudiBEAUTY*, October 2015. http://saudibeautyblog.com/introducing-cliniques-editorial-platformthe-wink/.

"Scale of the Human Brain." *AI Impacts*, April 16, 2015. https://aiimpacts.org/scale-of-the-human-brain/.

Shawn Achor. "The Happiness Advantage." http://www.shawnachor.com/the-books/the-happiness-advantage/.

Sims, David. "The Radio-Age Genius of The Message." *The Atlantic*, November 21, 2015. https://www.theatlantic.com/entertainment/archive/2015/11/the-message-podcast/417051/.

Sinek, Simon. *Start With Why: How Great Leaders Inspire Everyone to Take Action.* London: Portfolio/Penguin, 2013.

Sinek, Simon. Understanding the Game We're Playing. Filmed October 16, 2016 at CreativeMornings, San Diego, CA. Video.

Sisodia, R., David Wolfe, and Jagdish N. Sheth. *Firms of Endearment: How World-Class Companies Profit from Passion and Purpose.* Upper Saddle River, NJ: Pearson Education, 2007.

Solomon, Micah. "Did Starbucks Just Create the Most Epic $250 Million Recruiting Tool Ever?" *Forbes*, October 26, 2015. https://www.forbes.com/sites/micahsolomon/2015/10/24/did-starbucks-just-create-the-most-epic-250-million-recruitment-tool-ever/#4e9e804f7a5d.

Smith, Greg. "Why I Am Leaving Goldman Sachs." *The New York Times*, March 14, 2012. http://www.nytimes.com/2012/03/14/opinion/why-i-am-leaving-goldman-sachs.html.

Soft Skills Learning. "What is the point?" http://softskillslearning.ie/existential-purpose-meaning-philosophy/.

Starbucks. "Company Information." https://www.starbucks.com/about-us/company-information.

Statista. "Number of Red Bull cans sold worldwide from 2011 to 2016 (in billions)." https://www.statista.com/statistics/275163/red-bulls-number-of-cans-sold-worldwide/.

Statistic Brain. "New Years Resolution Statistics." Accessed November 28, 2017.
https://www.statisticbrain.com/new-years-resolution-statistics.

"Sub-Zero Announces Fresh Food Matters Initiative Highlighting Fresh Food's
Impact, Empowering People to Choose Fresh." *Sub-Zero*, April 26, 2016.
http://www.subzero-wolf.com/company/press-releases/sub-zero-announces-
fresh-food-matters-initiative.

Sweetgreen. "Our Story." http://www.sweetgreen.com/our-story/.

Taube, Aaron. "All Of Thailand Is Compulsively Weeping Over This One Life
Insurance Ad." *Business Insider*, April 10, 2014. http://www.businessinsider.
com/thai-life-tearjerker-ad-2014-4.

Team Rubicon. "Our Mission." https://teamrubiconusa.org/mission/.

Terkel, Studs. *Working: People Talk About What They Do All Day and How They
Feel About What They Do*. New York/London: The New Press, 1997.

"The Cost of Employee Turnover." *Zen Workplace*. October 28, 2016.
www.zenworkplace.com/2014/07/01/cost-employee-turnover/.

"The Boeing Co. Announced Friday It Will Ban Smoking..." UPI, February 27,
1987. https://www.upi.com/Archives/1987/02/27/The-Boeing-Co-announced-
Friday-it-will-ban-smoking/4699541400400/.

The International Business Awards. "Thai Life Insurance - CSR Program of the
Year." http://stevieawards.com/iba/thai-life-insurance-csr-program-year.

The Office of Hillary Rodham Clinton. "About Hillary." https://www.
hillaryclinton.com/about/.

The Wall Street Journal. "Demographic 2050 Destiny." http://graphics.wsj.
com/2050-demographic-destiny/.

Thorpe, Devin. "New Report: 'Purpose-Oriented' Employees 'Outperform."
Forbes, December 22, 2015. https://www.forbes.com/sites/
devinthorpe/2015/12/22/4988/#23c092813211.

Tools of Titans. "Intro." https://toolsoftitans.com/intro/#main.

Trump Pence Make America Great Again. "About." https://www.donaldjtrump.
com/about/.

Tucker, Ian. "Michael Acton Smith: 'We want to show meditation is common
sense.'" *The Guardian*, October 8, 2017. https://www.theguardian.com/
technology/2017/oct/08/michael-acton-smith-meditation-common-sense-
moshi-monsters-calm-app.

Turkington, Carol, and Joseph Harris. *The Encyclopedia of the Brain and Brain
Disorders*. New York, N.Y: Facts on File, 2009.

Uber. "Our trip history." https://www.uber.com/our-story/.

Van Mechelen, Erik. "3 Reasons Holacracy Didn't Work for Medium: A
Perspective from Octalysis Design." *Yu-kai Chou: Gamification & Behavioral
Design*, February 2, 2017. http://yukaichou.com/workplace-gamification/3-
reasons-holacracy-didnt-work-for-medium-a-perspective-from-octalysis-
design/.

Walters, Natalie. "McDonald's Hamburger University can be harder to get into than Harvard and is even cooler than you'd imagine." *Business Insider*, October 24, 2015. http://www.businessinsider.com/mcdonalds-hamburger-university-2333/#hamburger-university-has-16-full-time-college-professors-on-staff-in-the-us-with-the-ability-to-teach-in-28-languages-6.

WorldBlue. "The 2010 WorldBlu List." Awardee Profile. http://www.worldblu.com/awardee-profiles/.

West, Mollie and McCoubrey Judson. "Want to Strengthen Workplace Culture? Design a Ritual." *HuffPost*, December 6, 2017. https://www.huffingtonpost.com/great-work-cultures/want-to-strengthen-workpl_b_11730914.html.

Wittman, Andrew. "Stop Trying To Make Your Employees Happier." *Entrepreneur*, November 14, 2017. https://www.entrepreneur.com/article/302315.

Whole Foods. "Our Core Values." http://www.wholefoodsmarket.com/mission-values/core-values.

Whole Foods. "We Support Team Member Happiness and Excellence." http://www.wholefoodsmarket.com/mission-values/core-values/we-support-team-member-excellence-and-happiness.

Younger, Ben, dir. *Boiler Room*. 2000; New York: New Line Cinema & Team Todd, 2000. DVD.

Zak, Paul J. "How Stories Change the Brain." *Greater Good Magazine*, December 17, 2013. https://greatergood.berkeley.edu/article/item/how_stories_change_brain.

Zak, Paul J. *Trust Factor: The Science of Creating High-Performance Companies*. New York, NY: AMACOM, 2017.

Zak, Paul J. "Why Your Brain Loves Good Storytelling." *Harvard Business Review*, October 28, 2014. https://hbr.org/2014/10/why-your-brain-loves-good-storytelling.

Zawistowski, Mary. "Red Bull - More Than Just an Energy Drink." *social2b*, https://social2b.com/red-bull-more-than-just-an-energy-drink/.

Zimmer, Ben. "Wellness." *The New York Times*, April 17, 2010. http://www.nytimes.com/2010/04/18/magazine/18FOB-onlanguage-t.html.

"20 Years inside the Mind of the CEO...What's Next?" *PwC*. 2017. Accessed November 28, 2017. https://www.pwc.com/gx/en/ceo-survey/2017/pwc-ceo-20th-survey-report-2017.pdf.

"2015 Workforce Purpose Index." *Imperative*. 2015. Accessed November 28, 2017. https://cdn.imperative.com/media/public/Purpose_Index_2015.